The New

DATING

PLAYBOOK

for

BADASS

WOMEN

How to Go from

DATING SUCKS *to* WE'RE IN LOVE!

Faster and Easier

SCOTT MCDOUGAL

"We cannot change what we are not aware of,
and once we are aware, we cannot help but change."

—SHERYL SANDBERG

The New Dating Playbook for Badass Women

Scott McDougal

Copyright © 2020 Scott McDougal

ISBN: 978-1-7348546-0-2 (paperback), 978-1-7348546-1-9 (epub)

Disclaimer

Contents

Note to the Reader

Although you might be tempted to skip ahead at times, this interactive book *must* be read in chronological order. There are quizzes, challenges, and exercises throughout it, and you will want to know how you tested prior to moving on to the next section. Trust the process.

Introduction

TRUTH, LIES, AND LOVE

On July 24, 1897, in Atchison Kansas, a badass baby girl was born. Growing up in the 1900s, she undoubtedly experienced discrimination and disapproval, but she didn't let the sexist gender "rules" of her time dictate what a gal could or couldn't do.

She climbed trees, hunted rats with a .22 rifle, and filled her scrapbook with newspaper clippings of successful women in traditionally "male" fields. In 1921, at the age of 24, she took up aviation. And on May 20, 1932, she became the first woman to fly solo across the Atlantic Ocean.

Today, Amelia Mary Earhart is remembered as one of the great female pioneers in world history. But achieving her dreams didn't just fall into her lap. At some point in her life, she must've concluded that what she was taught to believe was not only untrue, but within her power to change. An empowering belief was formed, and she took action.

On December 1, 1955, in Montgomery Alabama, Rosa Parks decided she'd had enough with the "rules" of her time, too, and refused to give up her bus seat so that a white person could sit down.[1] Her courageous protest sparked the Civil Rights movement, which eventually led to the many equal rights advancements of the 1960s and well beyond.

Parks was committed to changing the traditional "roles" of black women and men, and her committed efforts forever altered our world for the better. The United States Congress has called her "the first lady of civil rights" and "the mother of the freedom movement."[2]

In 2014, Whitney Wolfe Herd said no to the status quo in online dating and founded Bumble, the innovative dating app that empowers women to make the first move. It's symbolic of a Sadie Hawkins dance where the ladies ask first, and a huge step forward in the push for gender equality in all aspects of life. Whitney happily shares how she and her husband met, and reveals their love story started with her unabashedly taking the lead.

All of these revolutionary women, and countless more like them, have three things in common. They had the courage to question the limiting beliefs they were taught. They explored better options for a more fulfilling life, and they took definitive action. These bold moves, while likely scary and uncomfortable at the time, greatly contributed to creating a better world—based on truth and love—for everyone's mutual benefit.

Do you have the courage to question the dating gender "roles" and courtship beliefs you were taught? Are you open to exploring better options for a more fulfilling love life? If so, this book will empower you to attract, meet, and keep an amazing man faster and easier than you ever thought possible, or to simply have a lot more fun dating than you're likely having now.

There are only two requirements to make this happen—truth and love.

If you do not know the truth about most men (and women) and are unknowingly basing your dating and relationship decisions on misinformation from your youth, it is nearly impossible to be a fully functional loving person. And no one wants to be with a person who they perceive as being unloving or closedminded. The truth will, indeed, set you free.

Once you discover the veracity about both yourself and most men, all you've got to do is shift toward becoming be a more insightful, integrated, and essentially, loving person—and your odds of meeting and keeping an incredible man will naturally increase. It only requires a bit of a makeover, not radical surgery.

The #1 Secret to Success with Men, Dating, and Relationships

The #1 secret to success with men, dating, and relationships is to more fully understand and appreciate your differences, and then work together for your common interest. But that's pretty tough to do when the majority of dating and relationship (and marriage) "experts"—including PhDs, licensed professional counselors, bestselling authors, speakers, coaches, religious leaders, and more—continue to base their gender beliefs and teachings on what I'm dubbing, "The Ancient Male Hierarchy Myth."

In short, most of the civilized world today still operates from a mostly false, outdated, and sexist gender standard. I invite you to replace it with a new dating and relationship paradigm I call, "Gender Enlightenment and Empowerment."

How I Stumbled Upon the Insights in This Book

Right about now, you might be wondering why I've written a book about dating in the first place, or more specifically, a dating book for *women*. You're probably thinking, *What does a man know about being a woman in the dating world anyway?* It's a fair question, and one that requires a detailed backstory to fully appreciate the unusual concepts within these pages.

My interest in dating and relationship coaching began more than twenty years ago, in high school, as I was clicking through TV channels and stumbled upon the dating game show, *Love Connection* with Chuck Woolery. I was mesmerized, and soon started watching *Loveline* with Dr. Drew and Adam Carolla, and innumerable romantic comedies. Even as a guy, I didn't care what other people thought. I was reading *Cosmo* and sex books and diving into all the pertinent knowledge in this field that I could find.

My goal wasn't to become a young Casanova. The topic simply grabbed my attention, stirred my curiosity, and drove me to learn as much as I could about men and women in romantic relationships. I'd never even had a single girlfriend, but I figured my preparation would pay off in the future.

I learned all about how to treat a woman once *in* a relationship, but I couldn't get past the first step—approaching the girls I was most attracted to. Secretly, I wished *they* would approach me—a memory that's extremely relevant to the insights in this book.

Finally, in college, I conquered my fear of approaching women and began regular dating. My "research" definitely paid off. By twenty-six, I'd gone from not having a single steady girlfriend in high school to successfully dating and winning the hearts of five incredible women (all in separate monogamous relationships), any one of whom I could've proposed to and likely received a favorable response.

I frequently received compliments like:

- "You are the sweetest, most romantic guy I've ever dated."
- "You text like a Hallmark card."
- "Oh my! Where did you learn how to do *that?*"

Each of these young women won my heart, too. But my career success was still very much in doubt, so I didn't feel comfortable enough to fully commit myself past the girlfriend stage.

When I was twenty-eight, an older woman I was going out with suggested I write books that would be helpful for men. She said I was super thoughtful, chivalrous, and boldly romantic, and that most guys are severely lacking in those qualities. I took her advice, wrote a few e-books for men, and received high praise from both men and women regarding the eventual products.

Here are some examples:

- "I have listened to Scott and I have gotten great results from his advice, because my special lady friend really appreciates the romantic gestures that I have picked up from his reports. Thanks, Scott!"—Dave
- "There were moments my heart throbbed with reinvigorated excitement that my dream guy and all I desire he encompasses truly exists out there . . . is it crazy that I will make every man in pursuit of me read your book, as sort of a front gate entrance to my heart?!"—Crystal
- "I would absolutely love it if my husband pulled the car aside, turned on my favorite song and we slow danced in the parking lot! It would be like we were kids again!"—Valerie

I, unfortunately, had minimal success selling my e-books. Writing and coaching were my innate strengths, not sales and running a business. I also made the mistake of trying to teach skills like "Creative Chivalry" and "Right-Brain Romance" at a time when most blokes were buying "Get Laid Quick" books like *The Game*. So, I ended up giving up on my coaching aspirations and resumed working my 9-to-5 job—writing advertising and marketing for ad agencies and Fortune 500 companies—all the while continuing my own search for the inner workings and mechanisms of true love.

The "Aha! Moment" That Compelled Me to Write This Book

Have you ever been convinced you'd found "the one," only to get your heart shattered into a million pieces? Or been married to the love of your life, and later watched it crumble?

I was thirty-four and had recently been through a tortuous breakup with my best friend and girlfriend of two years, only to see her jump into the arms of another man a week or two later, as evidenced by their pictures popping up in my Facebook newsfeed, pouring salt into my freshly broken heart.

In hindsight, she was darn near perfect for me, too. She was classy and sexy, had several gifts and talents I didn't have, came from a great family, loved me unconditionally, and made me a better man. If only I'd better understood not only our differences, but *why* we were different, I probably would've counted my blessings and proposed to her. Instead, I broke up with her and ended up missing her greatly.

When the stakes are high and you're considering spending the rest of your life with someone, it only takes one or two misunderstandings to sabotage what could've been "happily ever after."

Confused and heartbroken, I spent the next six months analyzing and replaying all of my previous dating and relationship experiences. Slowly, new insights and different patterns began to emerge. For example, I was always told *women* were great at communicating their innermost thoughts and feelings, and most men were bad at it. But looking back, none of my ex-girlfriends were particularly good at vulnerable communication, whereas that's definitely a strength of mine. The pieces were starting to quickly come together.

You were likely taught that *men* are great at initiating, making plans, and executing them with military precision. Has that been your experience with men, dating, and relationships? Or has that been an area of frustration?

A few months later, when I decided to venture back into the dating arena again, it struck me as odd that the dating apps appeared to be overflowing with smart, attractive, and in many cases, financially successful women. "Why are all *these* women single?" I wondered. There had to be an explanation, and I was determined to get to the bottom of it.

As an experienced copywriter for big brands, I used my professional skills to research as much as I could about the dating lives of dynamic single women, like you. I came at it strategically from a marketing perspective, pondering questions like:

- What do women really want in a man?
- Why can't they find the kind of guy they're looking for?
- What are their biggest complaints about dating men today?

Then, when I least expected it, I had the biggest "aha! moment" of my entire life:

> **The traditional gender "roles" and courtship "rules" that we were all taught to believe apply to all men and all women do *not* work for millions of men and women, because they do not align with the universal laws of attraction.**

As will be thoroughly explained in this book, the laws of attraction play a significant role in mate selection and countless dating and relationship dynamics. *No wonder millions of men and women are having such a hard time with dating and relationships, and staying married,* I concluded.

I *had* to find a way to share these breakthroughs in modern dating and relationship psychology for everyone's mutual benefit. But my work was cut out for me. Trying to change the long-held, widely touted traditional beliefs around dating and relationships would be like trying to convince a devout believer to give up or change religions.

Eager to help others, I began sharing my insights. I quickly learned I couldn't just come right out and rapid fire tell women how to date differently to make their love lives a thousand times easier. My convictions were too far off the current beaten path. Most women couldn't grasp my concepts. Worse, they flat-out rejected my premises, and offered less-than-pleasant feedback:

- "You are out of your mind."
- "Have you been drinking?"
- "Literally the biggest loser and desperate human being with zero social skills on the planet. Nobody likes you. Nobody. You're a loser. Get a clue."

They were unable to see what I *finally* could offer them, after more than a decade of extensive research and applied knowledge in everything from strategic communication and relationship psychology to the sciences of attraction and creativity, plus over fifteen years of personal dating experience. The insults just made me dig in and work harder.

But who could blame them? They'd held their gender and relationship beliefs for decades. According to Frantz Fanon, a psychiatrist, philosopher, revolutionary, and author, "Sometimes people hold a core belief that is very strong. When they are presented with evidence that works against that belief, the new evidence cannot be accepted. It would create a feeling that is extremely uncomfortable, called *cognitive dissonance*. And because it is so important to protect the core belief, they will rationalize, ignore and even deny anything that doesn't fit in with the core belief."[3] These skeptical women were stuck, yet completely unaware of that status.

Convinced the truth was on my side, I began creating a unique coaching program. A few weeks later, I landed a job as the lead copywriter for a company that owned and operated dozens of matchmaking companies—the kind that charge mature singles $2,000 to $10,000+ to make introductions on their behalf.

While working there for over two years, I had ample opportunities to verify my new insights, by reviewing their VIP female clients' matchmaking profiles, learning what types of men they were looking for but couldn't find, and reading their post-date feedback.

Everything they were communicating lined up perfectly with my new insights.

I was invited to speak at two dating service industry conferences and began privately coaching dynamic single women who already knew how to date the old-fashioned way, but weren't having measurable degrees of success.

From "Dating Sucks" to "We're in Love!"

My first three coaching clients went from getting asked out regularly, but hardly ever going on a second date, to meeting great guys, falling in love, and getting engaged. My theories were bearing fruit.

> What a difference one program can make! Before the program I was sure of who I was and what I was looking for only to realize that I had been limiting myself to what I thought my perfect match looked like. Scott McDougal's program taught me so much about mistakes I had been making in my dating life and opened a new realm of possibility for me by showing me that my beliefs in what a successful relationship looked like were wrong. The program has been life changing for me and I highly recommend this series to any woman serious about knowing more about herself and opening up her mind about what a healthy dating life looks like. Now, a year later and I am engaged to a man that I probably wouldn't have chosen before the program based on what I thought my ideal man looked like but I've never been so happy in a relationship and I am so glad the program showed me what true love looked like.—Desiree

Based on their results, I knew I had something special—the beginnings of an elite dating and relationship coaching program that several knowledgeable people in the field said could be worth $3,000+ per client. But I also wanted to potentially change the love lives of millions of women (and men), not just a few hundred. So, I decided to turn my high-end coaching program into this book.

What Qualifies Me to Teach This Material?

As you've learned, I am *not* a psychologist, a Ph.D., a licensed professional counselor, or any other traditionally educated gender psychology professional. Wait, *what?* This is, in actuality, an advantage, because it means I was not formally indoctrinated to believe "all men are like this" and "all women are like that." Instead, I have been free to think for myself and come to my own conclusions based on independent research and personal observations, *not* memorized indoctrinated gender assumptions and groupthink.

> "Once you're an expert in what you're doing, the best you can do is to improve it incrementally by ten to fifteen percent. But if you want to change something ten times or a hundred times, you have to challenge the foundation of everything that experts have taken for granted. You have to reimagine and recreate the foundation. And by becoming an expert, you can't challenge the foundation because that's what makes you an expert, or else you won't be an expert. Being a non-expert is the biggest advantage you have in terms of disrupting an industry."

—NAVEEN JAIN, BILLIONAIRE ENTREPRENEUR AND PHILANTHROPIST

I'm also a man—your target audience. Who better to help you fully understand the *true* nature of most men than a guy who's also spent much of his life studying male-female psychology in unconventional ways, which eventually empowered me to separate fact from fiction?

Speaking of facts, based on my personal experience talking to countless electrifying women, you are very likely a woman with a strong preference for formal research, scientific facts, and statistics. I will provide these here and there throughout this book, but in unconventional ways. It is exceedingly difficult to use "scientific facts" and "psychology best practices" to support innovative concepts, otherwise they wouldn't be innovative.

Again, much of what I've learned is based on my personal experiences, observational learning, and keen intuition, developed and refined over several decades. Therefore, I will be asking you to use similar methods—like your own eyes and ears, personal observations and dating experiences, logic and common sense—to come to your own conclusions throughout this book.

Why Am I Asking Women to Consider Dating Differently?

The traditional courtship "rules" do *not* work anymore and may actually be *keeping* you single. Most men already know *why* the current courtship "rules" aren't working anymore—because they're not based on truth and love. But they are powerless to do anything about it without your loving cooperation, because dating is best approached as a team sport.

As you will soon discover, as a woman, *you* are the one in the power position. But you cannot escape the universal laws of cause and effect, and neither can men. In plain English, your current actions and inactions in the dating world may be causing men to *react* to the way you are conducting yourself. If you do not like the responses you are getting, the fastest way to get better reactions and results is to modify your actions. By doing so, you will actively co-create an incredible dating life en route to a mutually beneficial healthy and rewarding relationship.

What to Expect

My goal with this book is to expose the mistruths you were taught to believe regarding most men (and women), to present a new perspective for you to consider, and to walk you through how to apply these insights to your love life throughout every stage of a successful relationship, including:

- Mate selection
- Online dating
- Texting, talking, and flirting
- Epic first and second dates
- Creative seduction
- Commitment
- Keeping your relationship healthy and strong
- Romancing his pants off
- Nailing special occasions
- Wowing his friends and family
- Getting him to propose, if that's your goal

Once you know the more accurate basics about most guys, this *New Dating Playbook* will empower you to go from single and frustrated with men and dating (and relationships), to quickly and more easily attracting, meeting, and keeping an amazing man you truly desire.

To accomplish this, we are going to be discussing a variety of subjects, from social programming and belief systems, to unconventional gender and behavioral psychology, brain science, strategic and creative communication, and more. So, get ready to delve into some eye-opening thoughts and concepts.

Final Thoughts Before We Get Started

"Learn from the mistakes of others.
You can't live long enough to make all of them yourself."

—ELEANOR ROOSEVELT

As you've already heard, my own love life has been like a rollercoaster ride, experiencing the highest of highs and the lowest of lows. My disappointments have taught me as much as my successes, and I am committed to passing the lessons on to you—*not* because I have all of the answers (I don't), but because I:

1. Love using my gifts and talents to help other people.
2. Hate seeing or hearing about people suffering needlessly.
3. Can't stand the thought of *not* sharing these revolutionary breakthroughs in modern dating and relationship psychology with women like you—and by default, men too.

I may not be the most conventional expert, but people who help change the world aren't usually traditional thinkers. They're mostly "ordinary" people like Amelia, Rosa, and Whitney who step out of their comfort zones, stand up for what they believe in, and use their unique skills, insights, and passions to make the world a better place.

My greatest desire for you is that by the end of this book, you will choose to take decisive actions and make your relationship dreams come true—for you and your future man. After all, love is a *choice*. But as you're about to discover, you may not even be aware of the many forces driving your various decisions, and your current power to change your dating destiny. So, we're going to start with the primary force that influences almost every decision you make—your beliefs.

Ready?

Chapter 1

THE POWER OF BELIEFS ON DATING

"The most common way people give up their power
is by thinking they don't have any."

—ALICE WALKER

Are you satisfied with the way your romantic life is working out? Are you meeting enough quality single men who meet your standards? Does online dating make you want to pull your hair out? Are men stepping up and pursuing you the way you want them to? When you go on a first date, do you usually get asked out on a second date? Have you ever been ghosted by a guy without any clear reason why? How many times have you liked a guy, but never took any action to advance the cause? When was the last time you shared a deep, passionate kiss that took your breath away? Have you had your fair share of serious relationships, but most have ended in heartbreak?

If you are not pleased with how your love life is playing out, and you have no idea what to do differently, please know that you're not alone in feeling confused and frustrated. But be warned: if you have no desire to try a different dating approach, despite the fact that your current routine is not giving you the results you desire, there's a distinct possibility your *current beliefs* about men, dating, and relationships could be sabotaging your own dating life. Thankfully, you can change your own beliefs and the trajectory they are putting you on in a short amount of time.

What Are Beliefs?

According to Richard Bandler, the co-creator of Neuro Linguistics Programming (NLP), beliefs are assumed or accepted truths:[4]

- Ideas we are committed to
- Deep convictions about the world, ourselves, and others
- Constructs we create to help us make sense of the world

Beliefs are clearly subjective. Just because a person *believes* something doesn't necessarily make it true. For example, millions of children believe that on Christmas Eve, a fictional character named Santa Claus literally flies all over the world delivering presents to everyone. I used to believe this myth too. The primary reason I believed it was because people I trusted *taught* me to believe it. I also *wanted* it to be true because it sounded awesome and beneficial to me. Once I was presented with a new perspective and new information, my beliefs about Santa Claus changed.

Your dating beliefs can be upgraded to better serve you, too. Beliefs are just that—ideas that we presently believe to be true. And because they're mere ideas, we can revise them at any time, once we have been presented with new information that feels *more in line* with our goals and circumstances.

Challenge: Dig deep and journal your current personal beliefs in regard to men and dating.

_____

_____

_____

_____

_____

_____

Examples:

- The man should always be the one to make the first move. I wouldn't want to come off as being too aggressive. Plus, that's his job.

- As a woman, I should not earn more money than my significant other because he might feel insecure or I might feel taken advantage of.

What You Were Taught to Believe About Men and Dating

As a young girl, you were likely taught to believe in a few fairy-tale stories, and even when you were older, you still *wanted* those fairytales to be true. For example, you are a beautiful princess and one day a "prince charming" is going to come along and rescue you. When that happens, you two will ride off into the sunset together and live happily ever after. At a very young age, this childhood story began to create a narrative for your future love life.

As you got older, this story likely evolved to include gender-specific "roles" and courtship "rules" for interacting with boys, such as:

- Boys should ask girls on dates.
- Boys should pay for your dates.
- Boys should be the one to initiate a first kiss.

Whether you realized it at the time or not, you began to form powerful mental agreements about how males and females are supposed to act in polite society. These beliefs likely led to more dating ideas about how males and females are "supposed" to act, such as:

- Males are active; your role is to be reactive.
- Males are supposed to be the primary breadwinner.
- Males take risks so you don't need to.

Whether these gender roles felt natural to you at the time or not, you likely went along with the program because that's what society taught you. Believe it or not, males were taught this forced narrative, too.

As you entered your teenage years and beyond, you likely used deductive reasoning to form other strongly held courtship beliefs, such as:

- You should never approach a guy first because men don't like that. You might make him feel emasculated. Or you may be perceived as being too "loose." If you really like a guy, just sit back and wait. If he doesn't approach you, either he doesn't like you or he's not a "real man."

- You should never pay for a first date because that's his job. If he's worth dating, he will always pay. It's okay to offer to pay half, but if he accepts your offer that's definitely a strike against him. He should also make more money than you because it's his responsibility to provide for you, not the other way around.

- You should never be the one to initiate a first kiss because it's the man's job to risk rejection. If he really likes you, he will kiss you.

If you caught yourself nodding in realization to most of these dating "rules," it's because many of your current courtship beliefs are likely based on gender stories you were taught to believe growing up. **The big idea you likely internalized is that in the dating world, men are leaders and women are followers.**

How Beliefs Impact Our Lives

Our actions mirror our beliefs. If you believe Santa Claus is real, you will think about him, mail him a wish list or letter, and maybe create a booby-trap in the fireplace on Christmas Eve with rope and bells that jingle in hopes of catching him so you can meet him, like I did when I was a little boy.

In dating, if you believe it's the man's job to pursue you, ask you out, plan and pay for everything, you will likely sit back and wait for the right man to do just that.

Whatever you believe, you do because:

- Beliefs create thoughts.
- Thoughts create feelings.
- Feelings play a significant role in our actions.
- Actions (and inactions) determine outcomes.

- Outcomes have a profound impact on our ever-evolving beliefs.

- And the cycle repeats.

Your personal beliefs about men and dating are extremely powerful because they dictate how you approach the courtship process. Sadly, many people are convinced that *their* beliefs are "right" and that *others* need to change their actions to accommodate their beliefs, even when it's clear this approach is *not* working. According to political psychologist John Jost, "People who suffer the most from a given state of affairs are paradoxically the least likely to question, challenge, reject, or change it."[5]

Examples:

- Tricia has been waiting eighteen years for the right man to come along. She's still waiting because she believes she has to sit back and be approached first, even though there have been plenty of men she's been interested in.

- Lisa's father was a dentist and made great money, so she always assumed her "Mr. Right" would make lots of money, too. She believed a man needed to make at least six figures to qualify to marry her, so she broke up with many amazing boyfriends—not because she didn't love them, but because she believed she deserved better.

Two Types of Beliefs

There are two basic types of beliefs—empowering and limiting. Limiting beliefs make it harder for us to achieve our goals. Empowering beliefs make it easier for us to achieve our goals.

Limiting Beliefs

1. "Life is full of disappointments."
2. "I'm cursed. Problems follow me everywhere I go."
3. "I can't change." (Or "I don't want to change.")
4. "I'm too fat or too skinny . . . too short or too tall."
5. "It is impossible to find a good, honest, and faithful man."
6. "Men need to step up and do their job."

There's no personal power—the ability to control one's destiny—in these limiting beliefs because they affirm an undesirable result, or avoid taking personal responsibility for one's own success in life. Instead of giving someone else that power, we have the ability to control our own situations through empowering beliefs.

Empowering Beliefs

1. "Life is full of opportunities."
2. "There is always a solution to any problem."
3. "I can absolutely change and have been doing so my entire life."
4. "I am perfectly imperfect just the way I am."
5. "Good, honest, and faithful men are all around me."
6. "I am equally responsible for my dating and relationship success."

Successful people choose empowering beliefs. Unsuccessful people choose limiting beliefs or allow others to choose for them.

Limiting beliefs don't just affect the people who believe them. They can also negatively impact others. This is especially true in dating because it takes *two* people working together to make a relationship a success, but only *one* person with toxic beliefs to destroy what could have been an amazing love story for *both* of them.

Why Core Beliefs About Men and Dating Must Be Reexamined

Let's imagine a great guy you'd love to go out with, and who's equally attracted to you. He secretly wishes *you* would take charge and ask him out. But because you've always been told it's the man's job to initiate, and that "real men" want you to sit back and do nothing so they can be the leader, you wait for him to formally ask you out.

Instead of asking you out, he decides not to because he doesn't have the natural assertiveness you've been told he "should" have. Meanwhile, you're left wondering, "What is wrong with this guy? Oh well, *his* loss."

Nothing happens and you two go your separate ways. Now you've both missed out on what could've been true love because you chose to sit back and wait, and he didn't know how to approach you.

There are plenty of fish in the sea, right? Perhaps. But what if this isn't just a one-time occurrence? What if misinterpretations like this aren't the exception, but are more the rule?

It makes no difference whether a person *intends* to misinterpret another person or not. Dating isn't based on intentions, but on the choices each person makes and the actions they take.

How Dating Is Like Dancing

Whether a couple is Salsa dancing, ballroom dancing, or line dancing, there's a beautiful rhythm that's created when both partners are moving together in synchronicity. In order to accomplish this, each partner must know their role—to lead or to follow.

In Salsa dancing, one steps forward while the other steps back.

One raises their partner's hand and the other goes for a spin. The more they dance together the better they get at reading each other's body language and dancing as one. Before they know it, they're wrapped up in the heat of the moment and having the time of their lives.

However, without a basic understanding of each partner's role and the steps each is responsible for, they can't even begin the dance. If he steps forward and she steps back, but she doesn't step back far enough, or he steps too far forward, her toes get stepped on, he feels like a stumblebum, and they *both* have to start all over again. If this frustrating experience continues, one or both dancers typically go their separate ways and look for a better partner.

If a person went dancing and this happened to them again and again, they'd be foolish to continue looking for another dance partner, then another, then another, while continuing to dance the *same* way each time. There's only so much blaming one can do before they realize *they* are the common denominator and seek out professional lessons to learn how to become a better dancer.

Likewise, if the way you've been dating isn't giving you the results you desire, you may *believe* men are to blame for not dating you the way you want them to. But what if most men are equally as frustrated with how you are trying to date them? What if you both hate dating because the social norms you were taught go against both your natural strengths and theirs?

Just because you were taught one thing growing up *doesn't* mean it is the best or only way to approach the dating game. As you will discover in the next two chapters, there are many different types of men (and women), and not everyone prefers to date the same way.

The first step is to learn more about yourself—let's get started.

Chapter 2

THE TALE OF TWO ENERGIES

"Self-awareness is the ability to take an honest look at your life without any attachment to it being right or wrong, good or bad."

—Debbie Ford

Have you ever wondered why you live your life the way you do? Or why the men you attract don't seem to live their lives the same way as you? The irrefutable laws of the universe could be a factor.

Science, through quantum physics, is showing us that everything in our universe is energy,[6] including you and me. We all possess two types of energy, which can be felt or sensed by others, but not literally seen. For now, let's call the first type of energy "Type 1" and the second type "Type 2." Different men and women have different ratios of both types.

Your energy mixology shapes your personality, body type, facial expressions, your natural strengths and weaknesses in most aspects of your life, how you think, what you believe, and how you see yourself and others.

Your unique mix also plays a significant role in countless dating dynamics, including the types of men you are most attracted to and whom are most attracted to you. Becoming more aware of these energies and how they impact social dynamics with men is crucial to better understanding yourself and the types of men that will bring you the most happiness and satisfaction.

What's Your Primary Energy Type?

The following is a quiz that will help you discover which energy type is dominant in your life, and to what degree. There are no right or wrong answers. This is simply a tool to help you better understand yourself.

After you complete this insightful quiz, we will discuss what your results mean, including specific ways they're likely impacting your ability to attract, meet, and keep the type of man you desire.

For now, select or highlight the adjectives in each column that best describe you. Not how you want to be perceived, or what you think you "should" be based on your gender, but how you live and function daily, especially in your career. Be honest with yourself.

Only choose one word or phrase per row.

DESCRIPTIONS OF EACH ENERGY TYPE

Type 1 Energy	Type 2 Energy
Straight Line Thinking, Tunnel Vision (Move from one thought to the next)	Circular, Scattered Thinking (Constantly analyzing and replaying)
Methodical, focused	Expansive, easily distracted
Goal-oriented (Just get it done)	Detail-oriented (Perfectionist)
Independent, Solo	Dependent, Collaborative
Take control of your own life	Focus on helping others first
Accomplishing things	Doing what is right or good
Direct Communicator	Indirect Communicator
Structured	Unstructured
More Extroverted	More Introverted
Driven, Work-Focused	More Laid Back
Orderly, Organized, Clean	Disorderly, Disorganized, Messy
Empowering	Surrendering
More responsive to needs of self	More responsive to the needs of others
Busy	Take your time.
Primarily Power-driven	Primarily Purpose-driven
Performance-based job, gets bonuses	Salaried job

DESCRIPTIONS OF EACH ENERGY TYPE

Type 1 Energy	Type 2 Energy
High Earner (Income of $75,000 + per year)	Average Earner (Income of $0 to $74,999 per year)
Don't like to write (Especially about yourself)	Enjoy writing (Especially about yourself)
Prefer to work alone	Prefer to work as a team
Competitive	Not very competitive
Left-Brain Dominant (Logical)	Right-Brain Dominant (Creative)
Impatient, Urgent	Patient, Easygoing
Lead with your head	Lead with your heart
Speaking (Great talker)	Listening (Great listener)
Tough, Firm	Gentle, Flexible
Assertive	Accommodating
Leader	Follower
You most value achievement, competency, efficiency, and power.	You most value communication, love, and relationships.
You're constantly doing things to prove yourself and to develop your skills.	You're constantly doing things to help, nurture, and support others.
Your self-worth is primarily defined by your ability to achieve results.	Your self-worth is primarily defined by your feelings and quality of relationships.

DESCRIPTIONS OF EACH ENERGY TYPE

Type 1 Energy	Type 2 Energy
You value objects and things (clothes, jewelry) more than people and feelings.	You value people and feelings more than objects and things.
Achieving goals and success is more important than self-expression.	Sharing your feelings is more important than achieving goals and success.
When stressed or upset, you prefer to be alone, shut down, and think on your own.	When stressed or upset, prefer community, open up, express your feelings.
Don't like vulnerable communication	Enjoy vulnerable communication
Have lots of physical energy	Have more mental energy
Prefer outdoor activities	Prefer indoor activities
More of a morning person	More of a night owl
Prefer to plan ahead	Prefer to be spontaneous
Prefer being in the spotlight (You like being seen.)	Prefer being behind the scenes or blending in
More of a doer	More of a talker
Get it done ASAP	Often procrastinate
Keep moving forward	Dwell on mistakes
Make decisions quickly	Cautious about decisions
Taking risks can be really fun	Taking risks can be really scary

DESCRIPTIONS OF EACH ENERGY TYPE	
Type 1 Energy	**Type 2 Energy**
Don't really stick to a budget	Budget carefully
Enjoy spending money	Prefer to save money
Love to eat at restaurants	Prefer to cook or get takeout
Like being in control	Don't like being in control
Don't like to apologize	Quick to apologize
Confident, sometimes prideful	Not as confident, humble

Next, add up how many words or phrases you circled from each energy type and fill in the number below.

Type 1 Total: _____
Type 2 Total: _____

Which energy type are you more dominant in, Type 1 or Type 2?

Next, to what degree are you dominant in that type?

- 43-50 circled from Type 1 = I am extremely Type 1
- 35-42 circled in Type 1 = I am mostly Type 1
- 26-34 circled from Type 1 = I am more Type 1 than Type 2
- 25 circled from each type = I am evenly split between Type 1 and Type 2
- 26-34 circled from Type 2 = I am more Type 2 than Type 1
- 35-42 circled in Type 2 = I am mostly Type 2
- 43-50 circled from Type 2 = I am extremely Type 2

People are not linear. Men and women possess varying degrees of both types. The point of this exercise is to determine your *primary* energy type so we can focus on that, because that's what matters the most.

If I had to guess, based on my twenty years of research on gender, social, and behavioral psychology, and the fact that you're reading this book, I'd say you're Type 1 dominant. If you self-tested to be evenly split, or even Type 2 dominant, you could still be Type 1 dominant because, as a woman, you have likely been taught you have or "should have" many of the Type 2 qualities.

Either way, you will want to keep reading because you are going to learn all about the different types of men, how to decide which type you want to date or marry, and the most effective ways to achieve your relationship goals.

Question: Are you looking for a Type 1 dominant or type 2 dominant man? Or a man who strikes a balance between both types?

Chapter 3

THE UNIVERSAL LAWS OF ATTRACTION

"You can hate me. You can go out there and say anything you want about me. But you will love me later because I told you the truth."

—Mary J. Blige

Have you ever wondered why you attract the men you do? You've heard the phrases, "Like attracts like" and "Opposites attract." But how can this be? Don't these two popular sayings contradict each other? Let's clear this up once and for all.

Despite what many dating and relationship (and marriage) "experts" believe and teach, "Like attracts like" mostly applies to *platonic* (uncharged) attraction. For example, based on the test model from the previous chapter:

- Extremely or mostly Type 1 dominant women (and men) are usually good friends with other extremely or mostly Type 1 dominant women (and men).

- More balanced women (and men) usually socialize with each other.

- Extremely or mostly Type 2 dominant men (and women) find and relate to each other best.

Of course, you can still be buddies with men and women who don't share your energetic ratio. But for the most part, when it comes to *same sex friendship in particular*, you'll naturally gravitate toward (or feel most drawn to and comfortable with) people with your same or similar level of energy.

Note: The saying, "Like attracts like" is frequently used in reference to sharing common values or interests, but that's *not* attraction. That's simply having things in common.

When it comes to dating and relationships, "opposites attract" applies to *polar* (charged) attraction—also known as the Law of Polarity.

According to Michael J. Losier, author of the best-selling book, *Law of Attraction: The Science of Attracting More of What You Want and Less of What You Don't*, "The law of attraction already exists in your life whether you understand it or not, whether you like it or not, or whether you believe it or not."[7] So you might as well fully grasp it and make it work in your favor.

Have you ever made eye contact with a man in person, or seen a man's photos in his online dating profile, and instantly felt drawn to him? Being polar opposites and having *inverse* amounts of each energy type is what actually creates that feeling.

Similar to a magnet, you may literally feel a strong energetic "pull" toward men with the opposite energetic charge as you. And you may literally feel a "push" away from men with a similar energetic charge as you, the same way two magnets of the same charge will not stay together no matter how hard one tries. You may also feel energetically "flat" or "neutral" around men with your same energetic charge, even if you find them good looking.

The Most Commonly Used Labels for Each Energy Type

Now that you know which energy type you are dominant in, and that all men and women possess both types in varying degrees, let's review their more commonly used names, so you can better understand what these energy types mean in a dating context.

They are:

- Yin and Yang
- Masculine and Feminine
- Alpha and Beta
- Positive and Receptive

- Mars and Venus
- Order and Chaos
- Ego and Altruism

And according to the Law of Polarity:

- Yin attracts Yang
- Masculine attracts Feminine
- Alpha attracts Beta

- Positive attracts Receptive
- Mars attracts Venus
- Order attracts Chaos
- Ego attracts Altruism

I purposefully used the labels "Type 1" and "Type 2" earlier because it was crucial for you to learn which type you are dominant in before I revealed their more common names, which could easily have skewed your self-testing. It's now time to fully reveal the key concepts behind this testing exercise and, in actuality, much of the essence of this book.

Type 1 = Yin, Masculine, Alpha, Mars, Order, etc.
(more "male-like" attributes)

Type 2 = Yang, Feminine, Beta, Venus, Chaos, etc.
(more "female-like" attributes)

If you tested as Type 1 dominant, then your innate energy—a *vibe* which cannot be seen, but is definitely felt or sensed by others—is masculine dominant, the opposite of what you (and men) were taught you "should" have, based on your gender. This means the men you will typically attract and be the most magnetically attracted to will have feminine-dominant energy (like me), the opposite of what you (and they) were taught they "should" be based on *their* gender.

It *is* possible for a masculine-dominant woman and a masculine-dominant man to attract and be sexually turned on by each other. When it does occur, it usually has to do with recognizing similarities in each other (like attracts like). However else this exception might be described, it is *not* the same type of attraction as when opposite energies attract.

If you tested as evenly split between Type 1 and Type 2 (balanced), in theory, you *could* attract and be attracted to men with masculine-dominant and/or feminine-dominant energy. But you will most likely attract a man who's more balanced, like you. According to David Deida, a leading expert on the sexual and spiritual relationship between men and women, "Your sexual essence is always attracted to its energetic reciprocal. Masculine men are attracted to feminine women. Feminine men are attracted to masculine women. Balanced men are attracted to balanced women."[8]

Note: From this point forward, I am going to write as if you tested to be somewhere on the masculine-dominant scale. But regardless of how you tested, this *New Dating Playbook* will work for you because it is based on three universal laws of human nature—the Law of Polarity, the Law of Reciprocation, and the Law of Differentiation—which we will delve into later.

In case you're feeling confused or frustrated, know this: Feminine energy in men does *not* mean they wear lipstick and carry purses, the same way masculine energy in women doesn't mean they have a mustache or a beard. But one's dominant energy type *does* affect their physical features, personality type, preferred communication styles, innate strengths and weaknesses, career choices, and countless dating and relationship dynamics.

FUN
FACT

> As you will see, the world largely considers women with the *most* masculine energy to be the *most* strikingly beautiful and/or the sexiest.

Truth is, you probably hate the idea of being called masculine in any manner whatsoever. These are just labels though. All words, in all languages are nothing more than labels we use to describe the essence of something. The only true meaning a word has is the meaning a person gives it.

In theory, we could create labels like "Apples" and "Oranges." You would be an "apple" and the men you attract would be "oranges." My point is it makes zero difference which words we use, but they must be different for communication purposes, because they *are* very different.

I am mostly going to use the "Alpha" label to describe your dominant energy, vibe, and demeanor, because it's pretty certain you'd rather be called alpha than masculine. And I will be using the "Beta" label to describe men with feminine-dominant energy. Being beta-dominant doesn't mean they don't have *any* alpha qualities. It simply means beta is their default trait.

I'm fully aware that for most women, when categorizing men,

the "Alpha" label may have a more positive connotation, and "Beta" may have a slightly negative connotation (like coming in second). However, learning the characteristics of each type and understanding the roles each was *designed* to play in human sexual attraction is what truly matters, not arbitrary labels.

Dominant Energy Type Versus Behavior

The most frequently asked question I get when my alpha female clients first learn how polar attraction works is, "Can't I be alpha in my career and beta in my love life?"

You can choose to *act* more alpha (assertive) or beta (reactive) any time you like because behavior, to some extent, is a choice. But you will never *be* a beta-dominant woman *energetically* because you cannot change your overall alpha-dominance. As you will discover in Chapter 4, these energetic ratio qualities are innate and fixed. The same is true for beta-dominant men. They can do their best to try and *act* more alpha, but they're never going to *be* alpha-dominant because their essence is beta-dominant.

The fact that you two attract each other will also never change because the Law of Polarity *cannot* be broken.[9]

"If you don't like something, change it.
If you can't change it, change your attitude."

—MAYA ANGELO

Why Opposites Attract: The Law of Vibration

When looking for a soul mate, lover, or future husband, you may have previously looked for a man who's very similar to you. But as you now know, opposite energies attract, because the primary purpose of polar attraction is overall energetic balance and wholeness. Your synergistic qualities and unity make you more complete.

In 1962, professor Hilton Hotema, a controversial author and thought leader regarding higher consciousness, spirituality, and ancient wisdom, wrote, "Science has discovered the existence of a universal principle that impels every atom of matter and every entity of form to seek vibrational correspondence with every other atom and entity of its kind and character. This principle is known as the Law of Polarity. The Law of Polarity is the Law of Chemical Affinity. It is the Law of Duality, expressed in mankind as the Law of Sexuality… All phases of Existence are divided into two departments, (1) positive and (2) receptive."[10]

You, me, everyone else, and everything else has its own vibrational frequency. We are bound by The Law of Vibration.[11] In plain English, polar attraction occurs because the positive (masculine, alpha, order) atoms in your body are seeking vibrational harmony, stability, and completeness with the receptive (feminine, beta, chaos) atoms in a man's body.

If you are an extremely or mostly alpha-dominant woman, you have an abundance of "alpha" energy, and may be considerably lacking in "beta" energy. This can cause you to feel like you're sometimes energetically "too masculine" or "not feminine enough" when you compare yourself to your peers.

Extremely or mostly beta-dominant men have an abundance of "beta" energy and may be likewise lacking in "alpha" energy. This can cause them to feel overwhelmed by life's daily challenges and unable to "get their shit together." You will learn why shortly.

The reason you attract each other is because you're both somewhat energetically unbalanced, and you both need each other to become your highest and best self. As we'll see, an energetic and vibrational balance greatly benefits both you and the beta-dominant man you could choose to date and be in a relationship with.

How Energetic Balance Benefits You

Have you ever wanted to feel more energetically feminine? Previously, you may have believed a man's "masculinity" would make you feel more feminine. In reality, it's the beta man's "feminine energy" that will make you feel more feminine, *not* an alpha man.

When sharing physical space with a beta-dominant man, particularly when making eye contact, hugging, snuggling, or making love, his abundance of "feminine" energy and energetic vibrations will be shared with you, giving you more of what you need to become a more relaxed, more balanced, and *energetically* feminine woman. And your abundance of "masculine" energy gives a beta-dominant man more of what he needs to become a stronger, more balanced, and *energetically* masculine man.

This is called the exchange of power. It is simply the opposite "exchange of power" you were taught to believe you "should be" looking for and experiencing. Again, you both need each other to become your highest and best self, and *together* you are the whole package.

Why an Alpha Man Is NOT Your Perfect Match

First and foremost, if you are an alpha-dominant woman, you are most likely not going to be energetically and vibrationally attracted to alpha-dominant men because you share the same overall vibrational, energetic charge. If you've ever met a true alpha man, you may have found his presence to be "too masculine" for you. Sure, you might be *physically or sexually* attracted to an alpha-dominant man, or love the *idea* of being with an alpha man. But energetically, you are much more likely attracted to beta men because the number one goal of romantic polar attraction is balance, and they are your energetic reciprocal.

Alpha men have many desirable qualities: confidence, take-charge personalities, a knack for knowing what to say and do, positions or status of respect. But they also tend to be arrogant, controlling, domineering, self-centered, work-focused, poor listeners, poor communicators, easily angered, demanding, and insensitive. They are often known for not taking the time to think about what their partner wants or needs, which often leaves women feeling used and lonely. Does that sound like the kind of man you want to be with long-term?

Have you ever watched ABC's "reality" TV show, *The Bachelorette*? In my opinion, almost all of the bachelor contestants are between balanced and extremely beta-dominant. Often there's one man who has a massive ego, is super aggressive, and does *not* get along with the other men—clear indications he is an extremely or mostly alpha-dominant man (e.g., Chad Johnson).

Trying to date or marry an alpha man is like having two dominant male lions in the same pride. In nature, this scenario doesn't last long because they view each other as competition for the females. The stronger of the two literally kills the other or forces him to leave the pride forever.

Similarly, in the dating world, an alpha man will typically view you as competition and a threat to his strength—because he desires a submissive woman, preferably one with feminine-dominant energy or who he sees as more balanced. Over time, you will likely fight with each other in an attempt to prove dominance and end up "clawing" each other.

According to Sonya Rhodes, PhD, a psychotherapist and expert on marital and family relationships, and author of *The Alpha Woman Meets Her Match*, "The Alpha [woman] believes in herself—but has some blind spots. She assumes that as an Alpha female she should be partnered with an Alpha male. But clinical experience has shown me that this partnership is at the greatest risk for divorce, because two Alphas will tend to compete for power and dominance."[12] There's only room for one alpha in a relationship.

FUN
FACT

We typically think *all* species follow the alpha male-beta female "natural" order. But for orcas (killer whales), one of the most powerful predators in the world, the females are dominant and the males are submissive. If a female killer whale *insisted* on mating with a more dominant male than her, she'd have a real problem on her fins, because there simply aren't any dominant male killer whales. (Another fun fact: Among lions, the adult male is dominant but the *females* do the hunting.)

The Top 3 Reasons Why the Traditional Courtship "Rules" Must Go

First and foremost, the traditional courtship "rules" are based on the alpha man–beta woman dating paradigm, meaning they were *designed* to work for extremely or mostly alpha-dominant men, and extremely or mostly beta-dominant women. They say the man should be the one to step up, take charge, and run the show for you.

But as an alpha-dominant woman, you may hate being controlled because you prefer to take the lead, or to at least have some say in the matter. Most beta-dominant men want you to be more in control, or to be a more active participant—a win-win.

Second, the *his-storical* courtship "rules" (e.g., bride prices, arranged marriages, "gentleman callers," and chaperoned visits) are at least 4,000 years old.[13] Their foundational principle was that males offer *wealth* and females offer *support* (e.g., cooking and cleaning, bearing and raising children).

That's clearly *not* the case today. Thanks to massive women's rights advancements and individual liberties since 1848, these sexist gender "roles" are mostly gone now. Marriage is still a contract, but the "terms" have changed in your favor.

"The future does not fit in the containers of the past."

—RISHAD TABACCOWALA

Third, you acting like yourself in your career and socially with your girlfriends, then trying to play the "role" of a beta woman in your romantic life is likely the *root cause* of most of your dating and relationship frustrations with beta men. It's too incongruous.

As an alpha-dominant woman:

- You are a more natural leader, not a follower.
- You prefer to be active, not reactive.
- You enjoy taking risks because you love adventure and a challenge.
- You are a go-getter; you don't sit back and wait for others to give you permission.
- You may be an excellent provider—a breadwinner.

These qualities are what make you *you*, and not simply who you try to be. You may not be experiencing the same level of success you enjoy in your professional life in your dating life because you're holding back from being the *real* you when dating and approaching potential relationships.

> "Always be a first-rate version of yourself,
> instead of a second-rate version of somebody else."
>
> —JUDY GARLAND

Maybe you secretly hate having to wait for a man to approach you in person or to message you first online because you dislike being reactive and prefer to take charge, being assertive by nature.

So why aren't you acting more like yourself in the dating world?

It's possible you've been choosing to hold onto your socially programmed gender beliefs in your love life because it seemed advantageous, natural, or appropriate to sit back and make the men ask you out, plan your dates, and pay for them—whereas you likely broke free from the *same* socially programmed gender beliefs in your professional life because you realized they were disadvantageous, sexist, untrue, and in your power to change.

You are probably not intentionally trying to have it both ways. It's more likely that you've been misled to believe you must try to be someone you aren't, to achieve the results you desire with men and dating. In reality, trying to be someone you're not is one of the *worst* ways to approach dating because it's nearly impossible for a man to love the real you unless you are willing to show him who that is.

This is a huge problem, but it's only *half* of the problem.

Just as you've been socially programmed to believe you must play a dating gender "role" that doesn't let you be yourself, beta men (and balanced men) have been socially programmed to believe the exact same thing.

The traditional courtship "rules" are hurting *both* sexes by trying to force a narrative which just doesn't fit, and this leaves both sides frustrated and unfulfilled.

Most of the tasks you may be naturally good at, like being assertive when meeting new people, making plans with clients or your girlfriends, and paying your fair share of the bill, you may *not* be doing in the dating world because you were mistakenly taught to look for an alpha man, and are likely expecting *beta men* to play these particular roles.

The problem with this is that many beta men find initiating conversations with alpha-dominant women, making plans, and trying to execute them to be far more difficult than you could ever imagine, for reasons that will soon be abundantly clear.

It's like Alice in Wonderland. Everything is upside down. So why don't you use your innate strengths and ask them out or approach them first?

A Fork in the Road

Now that you know *your* primary sexual essence, and how the Law of Polarity works, there are two dating paths you can take. But only one holds promise to take you from single and frustrated with men and dating (or confused and unhappily married), to the promised land where dating is infinitely easier and a lot more fun.

Path 1: Continue to date beta-dominant men (or even balanced men) the same way you always have, by trying to force them to be someone they're not, while you pretend to be someone you're not. Or attempt to date alpha-dominant men and feel totally unsatisfied and unbalanced in your relationships.

Path 2: Learn the key differences between your innate strengths and weaknesses, and those of the typical beta man. Then tweak your mate selection criteria and your dating and relationship strategies to align with your respective strengths, and work together with your date(s) for your mutual benefit.

Yes, it really is that simple! It is essential that you choose wisely, because your blissful future depends on it.

"When we become curious about the dissatisfying defaults in our world, we begin to recognize that most of them have social origins: Rules and systems were created by people. And that awareness gives us the courage to contemplate how we can change them."

— Adam Grant,
Originals: How Non-Conformists Move the World

Chapter 4

UNDERSTANDING YOUR DIFFERENCES

"It is not our differences that divide us. It is our inability
to recognize, accept, and celebrate those differences."

—AUDRE LORDE

As you now know, when it comes to polar attraction, opposites attract. Having opposite energies makes you distinctly different people, especially if you are an extremely or mostly alpha-dominant woman because your equal opposite is an extremely or mostly beta-dominant man.

Understanding your differences will empower you to adapt your mate selection criteria and dating behavior accordingly, so you can work together for mutual benefit.

Note: The higher on the alpha-dominant woman scale you scored, the more applicable the following information will be toward you. In general, I see and respect all as individuals or fellow travelers on the planet. Still, we do have many differences, and we actually travel better together if these distinctions are more thoroughly understood and appreciated.

Different Worldviews

The alpha-dominant woman's primary desire is strength. She tends to view the world through the lens of strength versus weakness. She likely feels stronger when she focuses on her own inherent value, which is why she may be somewhat self-focused and determined to become the absolute best version of herself.

In the #1 *New York Times* Bestseller, *Men Are from Mars, Women Are from Venus*, which has sold over 40 million copies, John Gray, Ph.D., says "Martians [e.g., alphas] value power, competency, efficiency, and achievement. They are always doing things to prove themselves and develop their power and skills. Their sense of self is defined through their ability to achieve results. They experience fulfillment primarily through success and accomplishment."[14]

Do any of those characteristics sound like you?

The beta-dominant man's primary desire is goodness. According to Dr. Gray, "Venusians [e.g., betas] value love, communication, beauty and relationships. They spend a lot of time supporting, helping, and nurturing each other. Their sense of self is defined through their feelings and the quality of their relationships. They experience fulfillment primarily through sharing and relating."[15] They typically view the world through the lens of good versus bad, or right versus wrong. They feel stronger when they focus on the value of the lives of others, which is why many beta men are more focused on serving others than helping themselves.

There are many dating and relationship behaviors the two of you—an alpha woman and a beta man—will likely interpret completely differently, based on your respective worldviews (such as strength versus weakness, and good versus bad or right versus wrong).

For example, you may guard your emotions because you think it makes you look strong, or you think vulnerable communication would make you look weak, or it simply doesn't come naturally. But beta men often think being emotionally guarded is not the right approach, or even wrong. Likewise, beta men do things *they* view as right that you may interpret as being weak.

Misinterpretations like these can wreak havoc on various interactions from evaluating each other's online dating profile descriptions to messaging each other, first date conversations and beyond. Because you probably don't want to date a man you see as being weak. And he doesn't want to date a woman he sees as being emotionally unavailable, or who's not okay with him being transparent, or holds some other difference of opinion or competing worldview.

Different Motivations and Values

As an alpha woman, you typically prefer to do things on your own. You don't want anyone's help because that would take away from your personal pride and sense of satisfaction. Most beta men are collaborators. They prefer to do things for and with other people.

I've heard countless high alpha women say a man should be successful for himself or love himself first and foremost. Again, you have entirely separate motivations in life. Neither is right or wrong; they're just different. Instead of trying to change a man who is innately very different from you, embrace and lean into your distinctions to become a stronger union.

Lifestyle Preferences

Have you noticed any patterns among the beta men you meet online, go on dates with, or have been in a relationship with? You may have noticed different lifestyle preferences, such as you wanting to always be on-the-go—exercising, eating out, going to concerts, or traveling the world—and them perhaps being more interested in relaxing, ordering takeout, having deep conversations, or walking hand in hand.

Many alpha women:	Many beta men:
• Have more physical energy, and often less mental energy	• Have more mental energy, and often less physical energy
• Are impatient and often in a hurry to get shit done	• Are a bit more patient, relaxed, and easy going
• Are more concerned with success and independence	• Are more concerned with altruism and community
• Are more interested in objects and things than people and feelings	• Are more interested in people and feelings than objects and things
• Love fast cars, bold fashions—things that express power and garner attention	• Find relationships more important than work and technology
• Think personal expression is overrated	• Think personal expression is very important
• Must achieve goals solo, because autonomy is a symbol of competence	• Prefer to achieve goals as a team and share the credit

Careers and Money

Our innate strengths and weaknesses, personalities, worldviews, and personal motivations and values play a definite part in determining the careers we choose. These attributes all eventually play a significant role in how much money one makes.

For example, extremely or mostly alpha-dominant women (and men) often gravitate to commission-based fields with nearly unlimited earning potential—such as sales, real estate, recruiting, business development, or being an entrepreneur and running their own business. Many are also managers, directors, and C-level executives. That's because Type 1 (masculine, alpha, order) traits like having a laser beam focus, a competitive spirit, a goal-oriented attitude, an assertive personality, an enduring drive to succeed, a preference for working independently, and natural born leadership qualities are huge *advantages* in these professions, and others.

Extremely or mostly beta-dominant men (and women) often shy away from these fields, or struggle to succeed in them. This is because Type 2 (feminine, beta, chaos) characteristics like being unstructured, laid-back, introverted, collaborative, creative, or great followers tend to be huge *disadvantages* in these fields.

Note: If a beta man is a standup guy who is honest to a fault and strives to never lie, cheat, or deceive anyone—all attractive relationship qualities—he may be at an even *bigger* disadvantage in the business world, because, unlike him, many people will do anything to make a buck.

Many beta men yearn to make a real difference in other people's lives, but feel trapped in a patriarchal society that expects them to be the breadwinner. Since childhood, society has been trying to force them to believe they must "be a man" and learn how to hunt, kill, and bring home the bacon. But that concept has likely felt unnatural to them their entire life.

Others *do* want to make a lot of money. But no matter how hard they try, their efforts often result in nothing but stress, fear, failure, and ultimately, shame. Because, again, their innate strengths and weaknesses are *disadvantages* in the Type-1 driven business world. And because many men are led to believe by general society that they're either a provider or a loser.

Note: These feelings of inadequacy can cause an amazing beta man to break up with the love of his life, solely because he believes he doesn't make as much money as a man "should."

A person who's naturally stronger in Type 2 skills and temperaments would be a more natural fit as a teacher, coach, counselor, writer, minister, artist, comedian, inventor, psychologist, or other

Type 2-driven profession, because that's where *their* skills are most useful and appreciated.

But don't make the mistake of thinking beta men are any less intelligent. Many beta men are extremely smart and hardworking, but they get stuck in a Catch-22 where their skills could be very valuable in a higher capacity, such as being the lead visionary of a cutting-edge company. Instead, they often struggle to get through the lower ranks and get bored, can't sit still, or give up; or if they butt heads with the alphas already in power positions, they often don't get the chance to move up and become a leader in their careers. Or they try to run their own business solo, but have a hard time because they prefer being on a team and collaborating with others. They may also go into fields like hospitality, graphic design, blue collar jobs, or public service. As a result, they are often compensated with lower salaries, *especially* compared to many extremely or mostly alpha women (and men). Nevertheless, there *are* beta men who do quite well for themselves. But it often extracts a toll on their overall well-being, especially if they push themselves beyond their natural talents and capacities.

Whichever career path a beta man is currently on, I can assure you he feels a lot of unnatural pressure to provide for himself, his dates, and maybe a wife and kids eventually. Even so, if forced to choose between helping others and helping himself, many beta men will choose to help other people, even to the detriment of their own well-being. Call me crazy, but putting others ahead of oneself seems pretty noble—a quality you may consider very attractive in a future boyfriend or husband.

If you are an extremely or mostly alpha-dominant woman with a thriving career, you can probably now better understand how you expecting an extremely or mostly beta-dominant man—someone who definitely helps balance you—to have the same salary (or assets) as you is not reasonable or relationally productive.

If you are an alpha-dominant schoolteacher, counselor, nurse, or project manager—for example—and you planned long ago to marry an accomplished breadwinner type, maybe you still will. *But the world has changed.* Women are making more and more, and men are making less and less. Expectations and reality are on a collision course.

Now that you know *why* you need each other for your mutual benefit and long-term happiness, hopefully you'll be more willing to make a few adjustments to your mate selection process and look for a man with the potential to *become* the man of your dreams with your ongoing support and encouragement. Or better yet, choose to love and accept him for who he is, and don't try to turn him into someone he's never going to be—an alpha-dominant man. You want a partner who loves and accepts you as you are, so that requires you extending the same courtesy to the man you choose to date. Again, all types have unique as well as very admirable overall qualities.

Different Brain Types

In case you are wondering *why* alpha women (and men) are so different than beta men (and women), here are some cutting-edge insights you'd be hard-pressed to find anywhere else.

Louann Brizendine, M.D., is an American scientist, neuro-psychiatrist, researcher, clinician and professor with more than twenty-five years of clinical experience, plus years of education at prestigious universities like Yale and Harvard. She is also the author the *New York Times* Bestseller, *The Female Brain* (published in 2007) and *The Male Brain* (published in 2011). According to Dr. Brizendine, "Scientists have documented an astonishing array of structural, chemical, genetic, hormonal, and functional brain differences between men and women. We've learned that men and women have different brain sensitivities to stress and conflict. They use different brain areas and circuits to solve problems, process language, experience and store the same strong emotion. Women may remember the smallest details of their first dates, and their biggest fights, while their husbands barely remember that these things happened. Brain structure and chemistry have everything to do why this is so."[16]

Dr. Brizendine is a brilliant woman. However, like most traditionally educated experts, her research is based on the alpha man–beta woman worldview—the *assumption* that most men are alpha-dominant and most women are beta-dominant. I'm claiming these gender characteristic generalizations are missing a lot of the nuances that underlie relationships in our rapidly evolving society.

Note: No one knows exactly how many men are *true* alphas (extremely or mostly alpha-dominant), but informed guesstimates are **5 percent or less** in the United States. **This would mean just about everything you've been taught about how *all* males are, or how they "should" be, likely only applies to the 5 percent of extremely or mostly alpha-dominant men.**

I believe extremely or mostly beta-dominant *women* could be equally as rare. As you will see, the scientific community says most people are more balanced. **This would also mean just about everything men have been taught about how *all* females are, or how they "should" be, likely only applies to the roughly 5% of extremely or mostly beta-dominant women.**

Therefore, it appears to me that much of what Dr. Brizendine has written and published about girls, women, and the "female brain" does not actually apply to alpha-dominant women. It applies more so to beta-dominant men. Likewise, many of her teachings about boys, men, and the "male brain" do not apply to beta-dominant men. They are more applicable to alpha-dominant women.

See for yourself in the following table with words and phrases which, according to Dr. Brizendine and several other experts[17] (along with my own personal experiences), describe the "male brain" and the "female brain." If you are extremely or mostly alpha-dominant, you will probably find that the "male brain" characteristics most likely line up with how your brain processes information. The "female brain" characteristics line up nearly perfectly with how extremely or mostly beta-dominant men's brains process information.

This is not a quiz. But feel free to circle the words and phrases which most closely describe you.

WORDS THAT DESCRIBE EACH BRAIN TYPE	
The "Male Brain"	The "Female Brain"
Simple	Complex
Strength, Ego, More aggressive	Communication, Responsiveness, Emotional Sensitivity
Competitive, More Sexual	Less Competitive, Stay Connected
Pursuers, Hunters, Chasers, Solution Seekers	Choosers, Reactors, Prefer Not to Make the First Move
Territorial, Sensitive to Potential Turf Threats	Gain Approval and Nurture
Work-Focused, Ambitious, Self-Focused	Others-Focused, Selfless
Take Action, Grab Whatever You Desire	Need Permission and Approval

WORDS THAT DESCRIBE EACH BRAIN TYPE	
The "Male Brain"	The "Female Brain"
Unemotional or Less Emotional	Emotional, Devoted, Nurturing
Decreased Interest in Talking and Socializing, Except in Sports, Sexual Pursuits, And Making Money	Outstanding Verbal Agility, Articulate, Vulnerable, Transparent
Self-Esteem Derived from Ability to Maintain Independence from Others	Self-Esteem Maintained by Ability to Sustain Intimate Relationships
Must Go Through Longer Process to Interpret Emotional Meaning	Nearly Psychic Ability to Read Faces and Tone of Voice for Emotions and States of Mind
Less Likely to Share, Take Turns	More Likely to Share, Take Turns
Plays for Social Rank, Power, Defense of Territory, Physical strength	Plays to Form Close, One-On-One Relationships
More Physical Energy (Less Mental Energy)	More Mental Energy (Less Physical Energy)
Higher Pain Tolerance	Lower Pain Tolerance
More Efficient, Need Less Sleep	Less Efficient, Need More Sleep
Compartmentalizes Everything, Sees Things One at a Time	Compartmentalizes Nothing, Sees Everything Simultaneously
Serious, Short, Direct Communication	Light-Hearted (Witty, Funny), Long, Indirect Communication
Win-Lose Philosophy (As long as I win, I don't care if you lose)	Lose-Win Philosophy (Okay with losing if I can help you win)
Taskmaster, Orderly, Organized	Go with the Flow, Disorderly, Disorganized

WORDS THAT DESCRIBE EACH BRAIN TYPE	
The "Male Brain"	The "Female Brain"
Decisive (Sequential Order)	Indecisive (Paradox of Choice)
Often Left-Brain Dominant? (Rational, Logical)	Often Right-Brain Dominant? (Creative, Emotional)
Results-Oriented, Just Get It Done	Detail-Oriented, Perfectionist, Dreamer
Impatient	More Patient, Peace-Loving
Planner	Spontaneous
Strong Desire to be Seen	Strong Desire to Be Heard
More Often Extroverted (But Need Time Alone, Too)	More Often Introverted (But Need Social Time, Too)
More Natural Leader	More Natural Follower

Do you see that the "male brain" characteristics are nearly identical to the "Type 1 Energy" characteristics from the quiz you took on pages 27-30 in chapter 2? And that the "female brain" characteristics are nearly identical to the "Type 2 Energy" characteristics?

As you will see, a person's sexual essence (e.g., alpha, balanced, beta) is actually their *brain's* essence.

How on Earth Did I Figure This Out?

"I have no special talent. I am only passionately curious."

—ALBERT EINSTEIN

In 2010, after many years wondering why I seemed to have more in common with what society said were "female characteristics"—like being relatively wild, undisciplined, sensitive, emotional, indecisive, and nurturing—I intuitively Googled the phrase, "Man that thinks like a woman." One of the top results was the BBC's Sex ID Quiz,[18] a diagnostic tool that psychologists use to determine where a person's brain falls on the male-female continuum *regardless of gender.*

The questions were more like those on the SAT test than questionnaires in magazines such as *Cosmopolitan* or *Seventeen.* For example, in one section, there were several sketches of a human face with different looks—smiling with eyes looking one way, frowning with eyes looking a different way—and I was asked to guess which of the five words listed correlated to that facial expression. Other sections were more spatial- and math-oriented. The quiz asked me to look at a series of shapes—such as six overlapping circles, or a large triangle filled with smaller triangles inside of it—and to guess which number below corresponded to the question. It was clearly an objective test.

After completing the quiz, my results came back: 100% FEMALE.

I was fascinated and felt a tremendous sense of relief. It confirmed my suspicion that I really *was* "different" than how society told me I was "supposed" to be. I never questioned my sexual orientation because I knew this quiz merely revealed how my brain processes information. That was a *pivotal* moment in my own self-awareness journey, and the tipping point that eventually led to many of the insights in this book.

A new paradigm was born!

Note: I must've aced the emotional facial-recognition questions (i.e., "female brain" functional strengths) and bombed all of the logical spatial-awareness questions (i.e., "male brain" functional strengths). A key takeaway here is that I can probably see things that you cannot, and you can probably see things that I cannot. And, again, that all of our brains function differently regardless of our gender.

In case you're wondering, *Should I go take that quiz now?* The full version of the BBC's Sex ID Quiz does not appear to be accessible anymore. You may be able to find a similar "brain type quiz" online, but it will likely only confirm what you already know. This *New Dating Playbook* reveals what matters the most—how to *apply* these insights to your dating life so you can quickly go from where you are now to where you want to be.

Do You Ever Feel "Different" from How You Are "Supposed" to Be?

As an alpha woman, if you've ever felt like you have more in common with what society told you were "male characteristics"—like being naturally assertive, work-focused, doing "guy stuff" like hunting, fishing, playing competitive sports, or getting your hands dirty and fixing things—it is very likely that you function more with a "male brain" than a "female brain." But don't panic.

According to a 2014 study by the University of Cambridge,[19] 17% of women have a "male" (systemizing) brain and 17% of men have a "female" (empathizing) brain. This statistic likely applies to *all* alpha-dominant women and beta-dominant men. According to neuroscientist Daphna Joel, "Only about 3% of people have a brain that is fully 'male' or fully 'female.' The other 97% of people have brains that are a mosaic of pink and blue."[20] This statistic likely applies to the *extremes* of each type. Most men and women are a balanced mixture of each brain type.

Note: According to these statistics, there are more men with "female-like brains" than "male-like brains," and more women with "male-like brains" than "female-like brains." Crazy, right? (For researchers: This could help explain why, on average, women live longer than men.[21])

To put these percentages into perspective, the U.S. population is approximately 330 million.[22] Using that as a basis, the 17% statistic translates to more than 56 million alpha-dominant women, and over 56 million beta-dominant men. The 3% statistics represents approximately 2.5 million *extremely* alpha women and 2.5 million *extremely* beta men in the U.S. alone. (The majority of the population is balanced, roughly 188 million people.) So, if you've ever felt "different" than how you're "supposed" to be, know that you are definitely *not* alone.

Again, the labels "male brain" and "female brain" refer to how a person's brain processes information, *not* their gender. There is, in actuality, no such thing as a physical male brain or a female brain.

These labels were likely chosen because, at the time, experts like Dr. Brizendine *believed* the gender stereotypes they were *taught* at prestigious universities, so they called stereotypical male thinking traits the "male brain," and stereotypical female thinking traits the "female brain." It's also possible they simply *assumed* that most men have a "male brain" and most women have a "female brain."

As they say, assumptions will get you into trouble more often than not.

> "If you leave assumptions lying around unchallenged and uncorrected, it isn't long before they morph into facts."
>
> —KIRAN MANRAL

The following chart simply shows that the words and phrases in each column essentially mean the same thing. Updating your lexicon will help you understand what these labels *actually* mean when you hear them being discussed, or thrown around—naively—in pop culture and "pop psychology."

"Type 1 Energy"	"Type 2 Energy"
Yin	Yang
Masculine	Feminine
Alpha	Beta
Positive	Receptive
Mars	Venus
Order	Chaos
Ego	Altruism
"Male Brain"	**"Female Brain"**
(Systemizing)	**(Empathizing)**

This can all get a bit confusing with so many interchangeable terms. The primary purpose of this book is to bring clarity to this subject, which will soon empower you to attract, meet, and keep the right man for you.

To learn more about the "male brain" and the "female brain," revisit my table chart on pages 55-57 or check out Dr. Brizendine's two books, *The Male Brain* and *The Female Brain*. Just remember to switch the perspectives to make them more applicable to alpha women and beta men when reading her books.

Interactive Learning: Fun Facts, Challenges, Analyses, and More

You may not be able to decipher a man's or a woman's sexual essence (e.g., brain type) simply by looking at a photo of them. But believe it or not, I often can. How? According to Dr. Brizendine, "The female brain has tremendous unique aptitudes [including] a nearly psychic capacity to read faces and tone of voice for emotions and states of mind." According to my Sex ID Quiz objective results, my brain is 100% female as it functions.

Further insights were gained by analyzing, replaying, and reflecting upon my more than fifteen years of dating experiences with alpha-dominant women. And doing the same with distant memories from my childhood and adolescent years. (Excellent long-term memory is a functional strength of the "female brain.")

Also, ever since my "aha! moment" four years ago—when I realized the traditional courtship "rules" do not align with the laws of attraction for millions of men and women—I have been intensely studying alpha women and beta men on TV, online, and in real-life; and using *pattern recognition* skills to connect the dots. It's not too dissimilar to how doctors diagnose a virus like the flu, for example. They simply look at all of the *symptoms.*

That's essentially what I do. I read people's eyes, facial expressions, body types, fashion preferences, written and verbal communication patterns, and countless other nuances to determine of a person is alpha-dominant or beta-dominant, including to what degree. If I can't immediately tell, a few strategic questions usually help solve the puzzle. In this regard, being an innately extremely sensitive, and detail-oriented man with "eagle eyes" can be a tremendously useful and valuable gift in this dating and relationship arena.

And I'm going to teach *you* how to utilize some of these same discernment techniques. Your dating and relationship skills will be greatly enhanced once you can identify a few key "signs" in beta men (and alpha women). Ready? Ponder alongside me with some of the following gender characteristic discernment exercises.

FUN FACT

There's a popular YouTube video with over 1.3 million views titled, "Men's Brains vs. Women's Brains," by Mark Gungor, a senior pastor and national marriage expert. You definitely want to go watch it. (Do so now if you'd like.) Gungor's analysis of each brain type is mostly in line with what I believe. In my opinion, however, the roles are reversed for alpha women and beta men. (Beta men *do* have a "nothing box" though.)

It is also my opinion that Gungor is an extremely or mostly beta-dominant man—meaning *he* almost certainly has an extremely or mostly "female brain." What makes me think that? First, he looks nothing like an alpha man. Second, when you watch this video, pay attention to *how* he describes the "woman's brain." You may notice that *he* is displaying clear signs of having a "female brain" *while* he's talking about it (e.g., emotionally very expressive, talking fast-and-loose). Third, in my opinion, his second wife, DeAnna Gungor, looks mostly alpha-dominant. Fourth, this pairing analysis aligns with the Law of Polarity.

All of this makes me wonder, *Does one of the world's most recognized experts on "men's brains" and "women's brains" have a full understanding of how to pinpoint which man or woman has which brain type? Does he even know his own brain type?*

FUN
FACT

In 2018, Hollywood turned Dr. Brizendine's *New York Times* Bestseller, *The Female Brain*, into a movie they *claimed* was based on "real-life science." Intrigued, I looked up pictures of the cast online. In my opinion, most of the actors playing the roles of men with "male brains" are beta-dominant *in real-life*, meaning they probably have more of a "female brain."

Challenge: Do a Google Image search for actor and comedian, Neil Brennan. Does he *look* like an overtly masculine, brawny, alpha man to you? He has videos posted online, too. Watch a few and reach your own conclusions. Is he alpha-dominant, balanced, or beta-dominant?

In my opinion, the actresses playing the roles of women with "female brains," like Sophia Vergara and Whitney Cummings, are very likely extremely or mostly alpha-dominant women, which would mean they have predominantly "male brains" *in real-life*.

Do you honestly believe Sophia Vergara and Whitney Cummings are *beta women*? Search for their photos and videos online. Do they look or act like stereotypically "girly girls" to you? Or are they strong, awe-inspiring, badass women?

Note: If my analyses are correct, it is *not* the actors' fault for playing these roles. They are actors, not PhDs. This movie would be a lot more believable, however, if the characters were more ideally cast.

FUN FACT

In both of her books, Dr. Brizendine uses examples of males and females who, in her *own* words, display clear signs of having the *opposite* brain type as the one she presumes they have.

For example, on page 53 of *The Male Brain,* she details a courtship interaction between Ryan, assumed to have the "male brain" (e.g., alpha man), and Nicole, assumed to have the "female brain" (e.g., beta woman).

She writes, "While Ryan didn't have that chiseled *GQ* look that Nicole found most attractive, he was cute and looked harmless enough. . . . While Ryan continued in pursuit mode, he took a deep breath as he quickly screwed up the courage to make his next move, desperately hoping this gorgeous woman was not out of his league."[23]

Does Dr. Brizendine's description of Ryan lead you to believe that he is a naturally assertive alpha-dominant man? If not, he very likely has a "female brain," not a "male brain."

You would think a woman with Dr. Brizendine's brain science expertise would *surely* know not only the differences between the "male brain" and the "female brain," but how to identify which man or woman has which type. Wouldn't you?

Note: Dr. Brizendine *herself* is very likely alpha-dominant (e.g., "male brain"). She says she was a tomboy growing up, so I believe she knows this. In my opinion, her husband, Dr. Samuel Barondes, MD, is almost certainly beta-dominant (e.g., "female brain") based on his looks alone. This pairing analysis also aligns with the Law of Polarity, which helped bring them together.

FUN FACT

I've been watching ABC's *The Bachelor* and *The Bachelorette* since its inception. Using my unique gender psychology insights and pattern recognition skills, I can often accurately predict—during the very first episode—which of the 25 female contestants or 25 male contestants will be in the top three at the end of the show, and often who will receive the "final rose." I don't need "Reality Steve's" help, either.

Challenge: The next time you watch *The Bachelor* or *The Bachelorette* (if you do), or any other dating show, see if you can spot which women or men might be extremely alpha; somewhat alpha; balanced; somewhat beta; or extremely beta.

Reminder: In my opinion, most of the bachelors are somewhere between balanced and extremely beta-dominant; and most of the bachelorettes are somewhere between balanced and extremely alpha-dominant. You have to look at how they dress, how they talk, how assertive they are, how emotionally reactive they are, whom attracts whom, and so on.

FUN FACT

It is exceedingly common for me to turn on the TV and see celebrity PhDs, MDs, LPCs, best-selling relationship authors, and other "authorities" giving singles and couples—usually alpha-dominant women and beta-dominant men—"expert advice" based on the traditional alpha man-beta woman gender psychology paradigm.

Challenge: The next time you see a PhD, MD, LPC, or any other gender psychology expert giving their analysis on TV, look for clues that they are basing their relationship advice or worldview on the assumption that *all men* are extremely or mostly alpha-dominant, and *all women* are extremely or mostly beta-dominant.

Again, in all likelihood, **5% to 10%** of all humans fit into this totally inadequate paradigm.

Truth: These present analyses of mine are not based on dogma. Like you, I was indoctrinated to believe the exact opposite of what I'm telling you. One typically doesn't abandon their core beliefs unless they experience overwhelming evidence to the contrary.

If you take a long look at world history, you'll certainly see there was never once a generation that wasn't completely mistaken regarding some fundamental concepts—like *believing* the Earth was flat, or not understanding that hands needed to be washed prior to performing surgery. Neither has there been a generation without creative pioneers who saw profound and legitimate truths that others failed to see. It would be naïve to think the present generation doesn't also fall into these same categories.

> "It ain't what you don't know that gets you into trouble.
> It's what you know for sure that just ain't so."
>
> —ATTRIBUTED TO MARK TWAIN

The point I'm making is that you should be exceedingly cautious whom you trust to give you accurate dating and relationship (or marriage) advice. If an expert has been formally educated and indoctrinated, particularly at the post-graduate or doctorate level in gender psychology, they should have tremendous insights regarding most men and women. **But in most cases, many of their gender *assumptions* will very likely be reversed. That's kind of a big deal.**

What Causes a Person to Have a "Male Brain" or a "Female Brain?"

I've read dozens of best-selling dating, relationship, and marriage books in which various experts take a stab at what causes a person to be alpha- or beta-dominant. You now know this is very likely the same thing as having a "male brain" or a "female brain." Throw in several other perplexing labels and confusion, indeed, reigns supreme.

Many believe these innate traits have evolved over the centuries. Some claim men and women can change their dominant energy type by improving their social skills, painting, exercising, or by meditating. Others believe environment and upbringing play a significant role, and that in recent years, society has endeavored to make "real men" more beta. You'll hear that in phrases like: "Men aren't men anymore."

According to Dr. Robert A. Glover, a PhD in marriage and family therapy, a leading authority on the "Nice Guy Syndrome," and author of the first-rate book for beta men, *No More Mr. Nice Guy*, "Five decades of dramatic social change and monumental shifts in the traditional family have created a breed of men who have been conditioned to seek the approval of others. These men are called Nice Guys. . . . They are happiest when they are making others happy."[24]

I believe Dr. Glover is correct, there *has* been an historic shift in social roles and the traditional family. I also agree there's been lots of conditioning. However, in my opinion, men (and women) haven't changed—not innately, at least—society has.

According to Dr. Brizendine in *The Female Brain*, all human brains start out unisex in the womb. "A huge testosterone surge beginning in the eighth week will turn this unisex brain male by killing off some cells in the communication centers and growing more cells in the sex and aggression centers. If the testosterone surge doesn't happen, the female brain continues to grow unperturbed."[25]

If this is true (I believe it is); and as you've learned in this book, extremely or mostly alpha-dominant women (and men) display clear signs of having an extremely or mostly "male brain;" then it seems highly likely that alpha females (and males) receive this *extra* boost of testosterone in utero, and extremely or mostly beta-dominant men (and women) may not get any of it (or receive the lowest dose possible). Balanced people likely get a medium shot of it.

Note: In general, males have significantly more testosterone than females do. LabCorp is a commonly used laboratory by the medical profession for many types of blood tests. Their reference range (normality) for testosterone in adult men is 264 to 916 units of measurement. Their reference range for adult women is 10 to 55. Those are pretty wide ranges, for both men and women, no? Where we fall within these ranges makes a big difference. In all likelihood, one of the main reasons that women (and men) fall where they do on the alpha to beta scale is significantly related to these respective hormone levels.

While I don't agree with many of Dr. Brizendine's assumptions about who has which brain type, I do agree that the primary factor that determines whether a person has a "male brain" or a "female brain" (or a balanced brain) is due to structural, chemical, genetic, hormonal, and functional brain differences[26] (i.e., branches of neuroscience), meaning we were all likely *born* this way.

This is why I believe you *cannot* change your overall sexual essence (brain type).

Let's take a small step beyond what is presently proven science. Based on my first-hand observations of thousands of males and females of all ages, I am convinced these traits are genetically passed down from mothers to daughters, and from fathers to sons. If an expectant mother is alpha-dominant and the father is beta-dominant, and they have a daughter, I believe she will inherit the mother's "male brain," making her alpha-dominant. If they have a son, he will inherit his father's "female brain," making him beta-dominant.

If this is true, you are an alpha-dominant woman because your mother is or was alpha-dominant, and her mother was also, and so on—*likely dating back many generations.* If you have a brother, he is most likely beta-dominant, like his father.

There *do* tend to be variances in the degree to which females are alpha and males are beta. For example, you could be mostly alpha-dominant. If you have a sister, she could be a little less so or a little more so. There's definitely a spectrum. But as a general rule, all of the women in your immediate and extended family will likely share the same overall energy/brain type as you, and the men are very likely to share the opposite energy/brain type.

Challenge: Look around. How many women do you know who may also be alpha-dominant? Your mom? Any sisters, aunts, daughters, or nieces? What about your closest girlfriends? Now consider all of the men you know. How many of them now seem more beta than alpha? Your dad? Your ex-boyfriends or ex-husband? Any brothers, uncles, sons, or nephews? It matters a great deal because these are foundational relationship traits.

In my opinion, many of the most famous men in world history were likely beta-dominant—including kings, emperors, presidents, prophets, visionaries and inventors, and countless war heroes. The most famous women in history were likely alpha-dominant.

Looks Can Be Very Deceiving

Don't be fooled if a man you meet looks or acts like what you *perceive* to be extremely masculine, because looks alone can be very misleading. He could be 6 feet tall, weigh 200 pounds, be a former Marine, and drive a muscle car or ride a Harley Davidson motorcycle—and *still* be a beta male based on how his brain processes information.

I don't recommend going out of your way to tell beta men that you think they are "betas" though, because most men are *convinced* they are alphas. It's a macho identity pride thing, and an eye-opening example of the power of social programming and personal beliefs.

I'm not saying you can't or shouldn't discuss this with your future boyfriend or husband. You probably should. But this may not be a winning first date conversation topic.

I did a Google Image search for "famous alpha men." There were pictures of guys like Ryan Gosling, Brad Pitt, George Clooney, Ryan Reynolds, Bradley Cooper, Johnny Depp, President Donald J. Trump, Michael Jordan, David Beckham, Will Smith, OJ Simpson, Denzel Washington, Al Pacino, Matt Damon, Robert Downey Jr., and Russell Crowe. Again, looks (and social status) can be *very* deceiving. I am *not* in agreement with this list—unless it was compiled on "opposite day."

Common Misunderstandings About Beta Men

There are many different types of beta-dominant men, just as there are many different types of strong alpha women. For example, beta men can be:

- Jocks and professional athletes
- Intellectuals, authors, and PhDs
- Firefighters, police officers, and military men
- Fashion-forward men and fashion-backward men
- Computer nerds and video game geeks
- Comedians and witty wordsmiths
- All-American types
- Tattooed bad boys with beards
- Southern gentlemen
- Surfer boys
- Good ole boys who love to hunt and fish
- And probably some players and jerks, too

Some are strong, sexy, and opinionated. Others are wild, spontaneous, and have almost no filter. Some are super witty, romantic, and charmers. Others are shy, nice, caring, and may have no idea how to even talk to a girl they like.

In short, they're the same men you've been around your entire life. They're simply wired differently, innately, than what you (and they) were led to believe.

15 Signs a Man May Be Extremely or Mostly Beta-Dominant

1. He is always thinking. His brain never shuts off. (Often labeled "ADHD brain.")
2. He is quiet and reserved at times, but also loves to talk and be heard.
3. He hates rules and is constantly challenging the status quo.
4. He looks like an alpha man in many ways, and is *convinced* he is one.
5. He loves hugs, kisses, cuddling, being romantic, and pleasing his woman.
6. He is extremely witty, charming, and funny. (May also laugh and smile big and brightly.)
7. He wears quirky attire that makes a statement (i.e., plaid shorts, pink shirt, red bowtie).
8. His home or office is extremely cluttered and disorganized most of the time.
9. He is a perfectionist and may be overly critical of himself (and you occasionally).
10. He loves helping others and is on a mission to change the world for the better.
11. His emotions are like a rollercoaster ride—up and down, and all around.
12. He is a great athlete and may have excellent hand-eye coordination.
13. He loves to play with kids (because he's a big kid), is an involved dad, or will be one.
14. His writing and speaking styles are repetitive and wordy. He uses two hundred words to say what you'd say in twenty words.
15. He is an ambitious, entrepreneurial dreamer type.

+He has dated, is dating, or is married to an extremely or mostly alpha-dominant woman.

In my opinion, these famous men are (or were) likely extremely or mostly beta-dominant:

Jordan Spieth	Marc Anthony	Usher
Russell Brand	Jamie Foxx	Drake
Colin Kaepernick	Jared Leto	Kanye West
Charlie Sheen	Mel Gibson	Magic Johnson
Tom Brady	Frank Sinatra	Eddie Murphy
Tiger Woods	Dr. Martin Luther King Jr.	Ryan Seacrest
Justin Bieber	Elvis Presley	Ty Burrell
Roger Federer	Robin Williams	Joaquin Phoenix
Matthew McConaughey	Tom Cruise	George W. Bush
Hero Fiennes-Tiffin	Tucker Max	Barack Obama
Patrick Mahomes	Chris Rock	The Trump men
Ashton Kutcher	Howard Stern	Eminem
Ben Affleck	Joel Osteen	Mark Manson
Joe Rogan	Jesse Watters	Gary Vaynerchuk
Mark Cuban	Chip Gaines	PewDiePie
Dr. Drew Pinsky	Neil deGrasse Tyson	Novak Djokovic
Dr. Phil McGraw	Aaron Rodgers	Lionel Messi
Leonardo DiCaprio	P.K. Subban	Kevin Hart
Derek Jeter	Tim McGraw	Jim Carey
Steve Harvey	Cameron Dallas	Alex Rodriguez
Neymar Jr.	Dave Chappell	Prince Harry
Lewis Howes	Jay Shetty	Elon Musk
Matthew Hussey	JP Sears	Pierce Brosnan
David Deida	Diddy	Jamie Dornan

Note: If you want to see a very likely *extremely alpha man* in action, search for the CNBC internet video titled, "The Profit: Standard Burger Showdown."[27] (You da man, Joe.)

15 Signs You May Be Extremely or Mostly Alpha-Dominant

1. You were a tomboy growing up, and you enjoy doing "guy stuff" today.

2. You love wearing bold, fashionable attire that makes a statement (i.e., attention-grabbing high heels, stunning dresses, ripped jeans, cute shorts, low-cut tops, tons of bracelets at once).

3. Your favorite colors to wear are white, black, red, royal blue, emerald green, or leopard print.

4. You frequently post "look at me" pictures and videos of yourself on social media and get lots of "likes."

5. You are extremely focused on your career, make six figures, and may be a workaholic.

6. You have what Dr. Sonya Rhodes calls, "Fifty Shades of Grey Syndrome." (You "secretly" desire an "alpha" lover who takes charge—likely the "vanilla" version of this movie.)

7. You strongly identify with titles like Wonder Woman, Laura Croft, Boss Babe, Queen Bee, Goddess, and Badass Woman.

8. You can be sassy, saucy, or sultry. You may have a "sailor's mouth" too.

9. You have lots of physical energy (relative to your peers), love to exercise, or look like you do.

10. You have had breast implants or other cosmetic procedures, or you desire to.

11. You have an insatiable desire to travel the world (wanderlust).

12. You are easily triggered and can go from relaxed to fistfight-like in seconds.

13. You are perpetually single, despite having endless opportunities not to be.

14. You hate being criticized because you hate feeling disrespected.

15. One or more of the items in this list pissed you off.

In my opinion, these famous women are very likely *extremely* alpha-dominant:

Alexandria Ocasio-Cortez	Rhianna
Angelina Jolie	Michelle Lewin
Eva Longoria	Hannah Brown
The Kardashians	Wendy Williams
Kendall and Kylie Jenner	Alyssa Milano
Nikki and Brie Bella	Demi Lavato
Gisele Bundchen	Aija Mayrock
Jenny McCarthy	Tyra Banks
Niki Minaj	Lori Laughlin
Sarah Hyland	Danica Patrick
Ava Marie Clements	Dana Loesch
Leah Rose Clements	Alessandra Ambrosia
Ashley Graham	Vanessa Hudgens
Bella Hadid	Ainsley Earhardt
Janet Mock	Angie Harmon
Elena Cardone	Mila Kunis
Susan Ward	Olivia Wilde
Serena Williams	Ronda Rousey
Yanet Garcia	Karen McDougal
Meghan McCain	Hannah Ann Sluss
Demi Moore	Julianne Hough
Megan Fox	Hope Solo
Jennifer Lopez	Misty Copeland
Melania Trump	Allison Stokke Fowler
Jessica Biel	Bridget Moynahan

In my opinion, these famous women are likely *mostly* alpha-dominant:

Selena Gomez	Lady Gaga	Salma Hayek
Diane Lane	Katie Perry	Kristen Bell
Britney Spears	Jodie Foster	Constance Wu
Sandra Bullock	Kristin Cavallari	Katie Couric
Josephine Langford	Melissa Theuriau	Megyn Kelly
Michelle Yeoh	Huda Kattan	Emma Watson
Barbara Corcoran	Priyanka Chopra	Paula White-Cain
Lori Greiner	Sheryl Sandberg	Nikki Haley
Ashley Judd	Michelle Kwan	Michelle Obama
Carrie Underwood	Greta Thunberg	Lindsey Vonn
Taylor Swift	Ivanka Trump	Sheryl Crow
Lisa Leslie	Tori Burch	Miley Cyrus
Mika Brzezinski	Oprah	Jada Pinkett Smith
E.L. James	Madonna	Jessica Chastain
Chiara Ferragni	Meghan Markle	Tulsi Gabbard
Maria Sharapova	Charlize Theron	Beyoncé
Georgina Chapman	Patti Stanger	Alex Morgan
Ariana Grande	Kate Upton	Gal Gadot
Shakira	Natalie Portman	Whitney Wolfe Herd

If you suspect you might be extremely or mostly alpha-dominant, again, the men you will find the most sexually attractive (energetically) will typically be extremely or mostly beta-dominant men. This means you will likely have completely different strengths and weaknesses, and brain types, which can cause a lot of unnecessary confusion, frustration, and conflict in dating and relationships (and marriage) if you two are not aware of your innate differences.

8 Signs You May Be a Mid- to Low-Alpha Woman

1. You laughed out loud while reading the *15 Signs a Woman May Be Extremely or Mostly Alpha-Dominant* list on page 75.

2. You have a few of those qualities too, but perhaps to a lesser degree.

3. You've ever had a Bumble dating profile. (You signed up to go first.)

4. You are tightly-wound, desire control, and may be a people-pleaser.

5. You are friends with an extremely or mostly alpha-dominant woman.

6. You are very attracted to extremely or mostly beta men, but may have a difficult time getting them to like you, because they often desire a woman with even more "masculine" energy.

7. You have an unfavorable opinion of many extremely or mostly alpha-dominant women (e.g., mean girls), but you secretly envy them some, too.

8. You wish I hadn't used the "Badass" in my book title. You would've preferred a sweeter, softer, more "feminine" adjective—or simply *The New Dating Playbook for Women*.

In my opinion, these famous women could be mid- to low-alphas:

Queen Latifah	Meryl Streep
Kristin Davis	Reese Witherspoon
Rachel Hollis	Jennifer Aniston
Sara Blakely	Drew Barrymore
Dr. Amy Cuddy	Jessica Alba
Marie Forleo	Halle Berry
Lisa Kudrow	Chelsea Handler
Brené Brown	Kate Middleton
Mandy Ginsberg	J.K. Rowling
Amy Schumer	Sharon Osbourne
Whoopi Goldberg	Jennifer Lawrence
Rachel Ray	Cynthia Nixon
Barbara Bush	Tina Fey
Angela Merkel	Amy Poehler
Joy Behar	Mindy Kaling
Julia Roberts	Gloria Steinem
Malala Yousafzai	Ruth Bader Ginsburg

Note: The *only* famous very likely *extremely* (or mostly) *beta-dominant woman* I can think of is Ellen DeGeneres. She's constantly smiling big and brightly; talking fast and loose; dancing fluidly all over the set of *The Ellen DeGeneres Show*—clear signs of wild "feminine" energy. Also, her wife, Portia de Rossi, is almost certainly extremely or mostly alpha-dominant based on her looks alone—game, set, *match.*

Now that you know so much more about the key differences between alpha women and beta men, let's take a quick look at some specific examples of how the traditional gender beliefs and courtship "rules" could be wreaking havoc on your mate selection process and dating life—so you can rise above them and make your own dating and relationship goals a reality.

Challenge: Look up Steve Harvey's book, *Act Like a Lady, Think Like a Man* on Amazon and click on the 1-star reviews. The most popular review, based on the number of people who voted it helpful, is titled, "What Steve Harvey wants, not what men want." This review demonstrates that many men (and women) adamantly *disagree* with the traditional gender views and dating stereotypes.

Please Note: If you're still questioning the insights and claims made thus far, know this: Most people's beliefs *don't* change overnight. So, you will probably need to give your brain adequate time to process these unique concepts. You are unlikely to agree with me on everything, but you wouldn't be the first person to read this material for the first time and think, *You're crazy, Scott!* Then, in a few weeks (or months), experience a few "aha! moments" of your own, and say, *OMG, he's really onto something here!*

Chapter 5

CHANGE YOUR DATING STORY AND CHANGE YOUR LOVE LIFE

"Step out of the history that is holding you back.
Step into the new story you are willing to create."

—Oprah Winfrey

The pursuit of true love should be about finding someone special with whom to give and receive love. However, it's possible you haven't been looking for actual love. You may have been looking for a man who fits *your story*—your idea of how your love life was supposed to unfold, based on the traditional gender roles you were taught to believe growing up.

For example, if you were born and raised in the South, and your dad told you you'd be wise to marry a Southern man and to stay away from Northerners, any hot guy you meet who's a Southerner, you may subconsciously gravitate to without realizing it's because it fits your "story." Or if you meet a man from New England, you may not realize why you choose not to pursue him.

You likely have several stories about who the man you marry ought to be, such as how tall he should be, or how much money he should make, even if you don't consciously realize the underlying influence is there, or have it written out on your dream "list."

Your personal *stories* are not necessarily right or wrong. But it's important to realize they're not set in stone, either. You can change them at any time and you've likely been doing so to some degree your whole life. For example, when you were a young girl, did you see yourself in the career you're in now? It's possible, but not likely. Your work story has probably evolved to fit your ever-changing wants and needs. Your "ideal partner" story should, too.

9 Stories That Could Be Wreaking Havoc on Your Mate Selection Process

As you now know, your mate selection process must align with the Law of Polarity, which states that opposites attract. You will definitely want to date and potentially marry a man whom you are attracted to. But being *too* specific about the type of man you "have to have" can work against you, too. With this in mind, here are a few common mate selection criteria to reconsider. As you read these, are there scenarios where you can be a little more flexible? Think about whether you were "taught" to want this particular story, or if it is truly what best suits your present needs.

1: The "Man Must Approach Me" Story

Thousands of years ago, in hunter-gatherer societies, we believe that most men did the hunting and most women did the gathering. Countless men and women have used these ancient gender roles to justify their beliefs that *all* men are born to "hunt" or pursue women in dating, too. But instinctually, this is only true for alpha men.

> "I can guarantee that back in the day, if a woman was left alone and she needed to eat, she would have to hunt. It's not biological imperative that says men have to ask us out; it's social conditioning. And we can change it."
>
> —Whitney Wolfe Herd

Have you ever seen a man you were very attracted to *freeze* after making deliberate eye contact with you? Consider the word "stunning," for example. We can truly be stunned in the presence of someone we find enormously attractive. When a beta man sees or meets an alpha woman in person whom he's very attracted to, her alpha *energy* will often stop him in his tracks, as if his feet were stuck in quicksand. This is especially true if he is extremely or mostly beta-dominant and she is extremely or mostly alpha-dominant, because the polarity between them is that much greater.

I promise you beta men don't choose to lock up. This can simply be a natural response, because "feminine" energy is *designed* to be pursued by "masculine" energy, not the other way around. Of course, many beta men have overcome their fear of approaching women. But others have not. And since it's not innate for either of them, *both* are capable of clamming up at any given moment, depending upon the circumstances.

Long after overcoming his fear of approaching women, Jason crossed paths with the most electrifying young woman he'd ever seen. The first time they made eye contact he *literally* felt a static shock between them in mid-air. (She is extraordinarily alpha-dominant, and he is extraordinarily beta-dominant, so the polarity between them was off the charts!)

A week or two later, he linked up with a group of her friends for a night of line dancing at a local honkytonk. He could not stop looking at her or thinking about her, but he couldn't make himself go talk to her. Next thing he knew, she walked right up to him, grabbed him by the hand, and pulled him onto the dance floor with her. (She grew tired of *waiting* for him to make a move, and her natural instincts took over.)

They shared one quick dance together because he was so mesmerized by her that he could barely move his feet, and he was embarrassed he couldn't keep up with her. (He prefers to Salsa.) Later that night, while ogling each other from afar, Jason desperately wanted to talk to and dance with her again. But the combination of their extreme polarity, and being in a loud club, and him not wanting to risk rejection in front of all of her friends, led to a whole bunch of nothing. They could've been soulmates. Instead confusion reigned and they never saw each other again. She probably assumed he didn't like her, but *nothing could be further from the truth.*

Tip: Most beta men are *not* intimidated by you. They're *drawn* to you. They simply want and need you to act and let them react because, again, that's the natural order for alpha women and beta men. What many *are* intimidated by, or simply fed up with, is an alpha woman's challenging courtship and financial expectations, which highlight the beta man's innate vulnerabilities and insecurities.

If you've ever really liked a guy and thought you dropped several "hints" that you wanted him to ask you out, but he never did, it may not have been because he *wasn't* interested. He may have liked you very much, too. He may simply have wanted *you* to approach him, or to initiate a flirtatious conversation, or to smile while making eye contact and literally wave him over to you, or to be even more direct and say, "I want you to take me out."

> "You've always had the power my dear,
> you just had to learn it for yourself."
> —GLINDA, THE GOOD WITCH, *WIZARD OF OZ*

Again, your natural instinct is likely to *act* and beta men's natural instinct is to *react*. In the dating world, this makes you the more natural "huntress" and beta men the "hunted."

It wouldn't surprise me if this one giant misinterpretation—the fact that most men hunted and most women gathered—was *the* foundational assumption which led most of the civilized world to assume that, in mating, men are "supposed" to lead and women are "supposed" to follow.

Your odds of meeting and dating a great guy will increase *exponentially* by learning and choosing to approach the men you're interested in, or at least giving them something to react to, versus sitting back and merely *hoping* a beta guy you like will approach you.

2: The "Man Must Be At Least 6 Feet Tall" Story

Historically, it's possible women wanted to marry men who were taller so they'd feel smaller and more protected. But today, you no longer need to hide from saber-toothed tigers. Good thing because there aren't that many men who are at least six-feet tall.

According to Malcolm Gladwell, *New Yorker* journalist, author, and speaker, 14.5% of all men in the United States are 6 feet or taller.[28] That's *all men*, not all single men. Roughly 3.9% of men are 6 foot 2 inches or taller. However, a significant number of women have been socially programmed to believe they must have a guy who's at least 6 feet tall. Based on the math, only a small percentage of women accomplish this goal, and many would be wise to consider tweaking this "requirement" a little bit.

Yara is an attractive, successful woman in her late thirties who's just 5 feet tall. She's petite, but with an alpha attitude and glowing personality like you wouldn't believe, and she won't date a man seriously who isn't at least 6'2". She no more needs a man who's 6'2" than she needs to fly to the moon. At 5 foot nothing, she could date and marry a man who's 5'8" or 5'10" and *even* if she wears 6-inch heels, he'd still be taller than her. But she's holding onto her irrational height requirement, and passing up a lot of great guys. Dating mindsets can really get in the way.

You don't even need a man who's taller than you. Many women date and marry men who are the same height or shorter, and enjoy fantastic love lives together, like Nicole Kidman (very likely alpha) and Keith Urban (very likely beta). If you happen to meet a tall guy and fall in love, great. But you could be just as happy with a man who's two inches taller than you, the same height as you, or two inches shorter than you.

3: The "Man Must Make More Money Than Me" Story

Women have different reasons for wanting to be with a man who makes the same as her or more. Some women view a man's financial success as evidence of more important qualities, like him being motivated, disciplined, educated, and driven. For others, it's about a feeling of safety and security knowing her income is more supplementary, not just for survival.

Some women believe the man should handle more of the financial load simply because he's a man. They don't want to be anyone's sugar momma. Others have the opposite problem. The men they meet are insecure about not being the breadwinner, and may even begrudge her for "making" him feel like less of a man. This view is probably more common among older generations of men (those in their late forties, fifties, and sixties) because they grew up in a time when women's rights weren't yet as advanced and mainstream, and women didn't have the earning power that they do now.

For other women, being with an equally successful man has more to do with overall compatibility and having similar financial goals and abilities, which is totally understandable, especially considering your social programming. *But the world has changed.* Women today—likely alpha women, in particular—enjoy more financial success and opportunities than ever before. And due to the Law of Cause and Effect (i.e., the seesaw effect), men—likely beta men, in particular—are making less and less. **This has created a much-needed shift in dating roles and responsibilities.**

Saying, "I want to be with a man who makes more money than me," is no different than saying, "Men should make more money than women simply because they're men." But is that not what you are passionately *against* in the business world? I'm pretty sure it is. **How is a man supposed to *not* make more than you in the business world, simply because he's a man, yet somehow make more money than you in the dating world, simply because he's a man?** They're both the same world and the more women fight to further gender equality and/or equal opportunity in the workforce, the harder it's going to get to find a man that makes more money than you, or even the same as you.

Question to Ponder: If you make significantly more money than the men you attract, shouldn't you be *celebrating?* Since 1848, women's rights pioneers like Susan B. Anthony and Elizabeth Cady Stanton have been fighting for the opportunities that *you* enjoy today. That's a great achievement! Furthermore, consider the *her-storical* significance of what you've helped to accomplish. Years from now, you, and badass career women like you, will be championed for being part of the first generation of women *in modern history* to upset the patriarchy, and to lead the way toward a matriarchy. As far as dating and relationships go, you may *already* be living in a matriarchy. That may or may not have been your intent, but it's a reality *you* helped to create!

4: The "Traditional Family Household" Story

> "What the world needs now is more women at work
> and more dads at home."
>
> —GLORIA STEINEM

Many adult alpha women likely suffer from "mommy guilt." They were "supposed" to raise a family but focused on their career instead. Many beta men suffer from "breadwinner shame." They were "supposed" to be the main provider. But for one reason or another, it never happened no matter how hard they tried.

Many beta men also love children and would relish the opportunity to be a stay-at-home dad. It seems to me there's an excellent compromise here: alpha woman has a baby and goes back to work, her passion; dad is the main caregiver and works part-time, or whatever a couple agrees on.

Note: This new family dynamic would likely be best for the women's movement, the men's movement, and the children, too—a win-win-win.

> "Strange new problems are being reported in the growing generations of children whose mothers were always there, driving them around, helping them with their homework—an inability to endure pain or discipline or pursue any self-sustained goal of any sort, a devastating boredom with life."
>
> —BETTY FRIEDAN

In 1981, Betty Freidan, the first president of the National Organization for Women (NOW) and author of *The Feminine Mystique* and *The Second Stage*, proposed that the liberation of men would be needed to complete the liberation of women. I agree. By freeing men (beta men in particular) from the courtship and financial expectations of the alpha man-beta woman worldview, and continuing to empower women in the workforce, women will flourish more and more for everyone's mutual benefit, provided women *share* their resources with men.

You're probably thinking, *Why would this be better for the children?*

It is well known and documented that generations of grown men, likely betas, were raised primarily by their moms, likely alphas, who did EVERYTHING for them (also known as helicopter moms), partly because dad was busy doing the breadwinning, and partly because most alpha women need to be needed and most beta boys want to be helped. I call this the **"Parenting Perfect Storm."**

In the wild, if an animal's mom (or dad) feeds them their entire youth, instead of teaching them how to hunt for themselves, then says, "You're an adult now, go make it on your own," that animal will *die* of starvation. Similarly, many beta men—*already* at a distinct disadvantage in the business world—were coddled by their mothers growing up, and then told, "Go make us proud." The result is often a "failure to launch." It's *not* their fault if one or both parents "clipped their wings," but they are definitely paying the price today. (This is just one of many factors that has contributed to "the fall of beta men" and "the rise of alpha women.")

By switching primary parenting roles, or co-parenting, again, an alpha mom can dedicate herself more to her career (if she desires to). A beta dad can spend more time focused on others—their kids—often his preference. And their kids—beta sons, in particular—will have to learn to be more independent, because most beta men have little desire to micromanage. So, alpha woman, if you are a breadwinner type, consider prioritizing finding a great beta man who loves children; can cook; would happily help out more around the house; maybe prepare a hot bath for you when you return from work; and add a lot more value to your life.

Progressive Thought for Feminists

In my opinion, the biggest key to ending *misogyny*, defined as "a hatred of women"[29] (i.e., discrimination against women), is to fight equally as hard, publicly, to end *misandry*, defined as "a hatred of men"[30] (i.e., discrimination against men), including any use of the phrase, "It's the man's job to . . ." Misogyny and misandry are almost certainly intrinsically linked, and, due to the Law of Reciprocation, very likely feed off each other in mutually destructive ways.

"Darkness cannot drive out darkness; only light can do that. Hate cannot drive out hate; only love can do that."

—Dr. Martin Luther King Jr.

By becoming more aware of the *actual* differences between various types of women and men, and working together to reverse the curse of the alpha man–beta woman paradigm, mutual love and respect can be restored for everyone's mutual benefit. **As an alpha (or balanced) woman, *you* can be a catalyst by implementing this *New Dating Playbook.***

Note for the Research Community

I am convinced that the liberation of alpha women and beta men from the alpha man–beta woman worldview (aided by this book) is a KEY component in solving, or at least alleviating, many pressing societal issues that are increasingly plaguing the Western world. If you have a growth mindset and you'd like to consult with me, please reach out. I truly believe the collective value of the insights in this book far exceeds the realm of dating and relationships alone.

"We cannot solve our problems with the same thinking we used when we created them."

—Albert Einstein

5: The "He Must Be Older than Me" Story

Traditionally, men prefer younger women and women prefer older men. But the opposite is often true for alpha women and beta men. If a man expresses a sincere interest in dating you, and you worry he's too young for you, know that just because you're five, ten, or even fifteen years older than him, it doesn't mean he thinks you're too old for him.

Maybe he's mature for his age and has always preferred women a few years older than him. Maybe he's going through a "fun" phase and likes the idea of being "taught" a few things. Maybe he's a charming gentleman who finds mature women to be more challenging and sexually confident. Or maybe you're simply the exception to the "rule"—he just likes you and doesn't care what age range society says is "acceptable" for him to date in.

These same scenarios are possible for you, too. Maybe you've always been more attracted to younger men for any number of reasons. Whether you feel energized by their youth; or find they're better able to keep up with you; or you're recently divorced and going through a "fun" stage of your own; you are free to date, be in a relationship with, and potentially marry whomever you'd like.

If you are concerned about being labeled a "cougar" or a "cradle robber," either date within your "appropriate" age range, or give the peanut gallery the middle finger salute and *you do you*. Whom you choose to date and be in a relationship with is none of their business. It's also possible people might stare at you and a younger man because you two are a dynamic couple; the women are envious of you; and the men are jealous of him. So be it.

The only scenario that *can* be a deal breaker for one or both of you is the biological factor when it comes to having children. If he's thirty-five and wants kids of his own someday, and you're forty-five, that could prevent him from seeing you as marriage material.

But it's also possible you're a single mom and he might not even want to have his own kids. He may be perfectly happy loving you and becoming an "insta-dad." If you make good money, he can also be at peace knowing he doesn't have to provide for a family all on his own. The reverse could also be true. If your childbearing "timeclock" has expired and you always wanted kids, or you love kids but didn't want to have your own, you could date and marry a single dad and become an "insta-mom."

6: The "My Religion Says It's His Job to Lead" Story

If you are religious now, or had a religious upbringing, I can see how this story could be viewed as problematic. After all, most religions are male-centric hierarchies with conservative views about the woman's "place" in relationships. The general consensus is men are leaders, and women are traditionally more submissive.

Since I was raised in the Christian tradition, and live in the South, I am aware that some single women use the Bible to justify playing a submissive role in dating and relationships. However, this choice may very well be doing more to keep them single than to help them enter into a loving relationship.

The main verse many Christians use to defend this belief is Ephesians 5:22–23. The King James Version reads, "Wives, submit yourselves unto your own husbands, as unto the Lord. For the husband is the head of the wife, even as Christ is the head of the church."

First and foremost, this text was written *thousands* of years ago, during a time when women were clearly considered and treated as second-class citizens. This makes it primarily based similarly to the alpha man–beta woman paradigm, but that degree of shackles is long gone.

Undoubtedly, many of the dozens of men who wrote the Bible were very likely beta (or balanced) men. Furthermore, in my opinion, Jesus himself was very likely beta-dominant. (He was a teacher who lived to love and serve others; adored children; spoke indirectly, in parables; broke the "rules" and rejected the status quo, and *willingly* paid the ultimate price for doing so.) Samson and Goliath were surely alphas.

Second, Ephesians 5:21 says, "Submit to one another out of reverence for Christ." This seems much more in line with what many Christians today practice—*equal partnerships.*

Third, even if you agree with the traditional interpretation of Ephesians 5:22–23, these verses *only* talk about *husbands and wives.* In case you're thinking this could or should be applied to dating, I've consulted several fundamentalist, conservative pastors and theologians, and they *all* told me there's no "transfer of authority" to the husband until they're officially married. These verses also don't say anything about single men having to ask single women out, plan and pay for dates, or to be the breadwinner.

In my opinion, any religious leader who loosely translates the Bible to say, "Men should play the role of the leader in courtship and dating" is simply using their social programming and cultural conditioning to justify making sexist assumptions based on the customs of married couples thousands of years ago. Even back then, many men didn't approach their future wives. Their families chose for them and made "arrangements."

It's also possible you (or they) may be guilty of *confirmation bias*, which is defined as "favoring information that confirms your previously existing beliefs or biases."[31] For example, if a woman believes it's the man's job to lead, she *could* locate one or two Bible verses that *might* support that position, and *ignore* all other verses that say otherwise, such as:

- "Faith without action is dead," (James 2:14–26). Prayer is great, but take physical action too.

- "The LORD God said, It is not good for the man to be alone. I will make him a helper suitable for him," (Genesis 2:18). Helpers help each other in all aspects of life. As an alpha woman, you are also the most suitable helper for a beta man.

- "Do unto others as you would have them do unto you," (Luke 6:31). The Golden Rule is also found in nearly every world religion.

- "Each of you should look not only to your own interests, but also to the interests of others," (Philippians 2:4).

- You reap what you sow (Galatians 6:7–9). The concept of Karma (i.e., the Law of Cause and Effect, the Law of Reciprocation) is discussed in nearly every world religion, too.

- "It is more blessed to give than to receive," (Acts 20:35).

- "Love is patient, love is kind . . . it is not self-seeking," (1 Corinthians 13:4–5).

- Help those less fortunate than you (Leviticus 25:35; Deuteronomy 15:7–8, 10–11; Proverbs 22:22–23; James 2:2–4).

These all emphasize *partnerships*, being selfless, and using one's inherent gifts and talents to love and serve others. Some or all of these points may also be applicable to dating today, whether you identify as Christian or practice Judaism, Hinduism, Islam, Buddhism, Taoism, Sikhism, Agnosticism, or even Atheism. **The key is to be aware of your biases and consider whether you still believe them to be true.**

Quick Fix

If my using the word "leader" (or "co-leader") to describe a woman in a dating context makes you uncomfortable, then pick a different label. For example, you will be an action-taker, and I will show you how to get men to take more action. You'll simply be using your God-given gifts to help a man become a better leader for your mutual benefit as a couple.

In an ideal relationship, the person with the greatest gifts or strengths in a particular arena should be the leader in that regard. If you are a go-getter in your career, then be a go-getter in your dating life. If you are a natural planner, then you might want to plan more of your dates. If you are great with numbers and organization, and your boyfriend (or husband) is not, then you should probably be managing the checkbook and finances.

In summary, be yourself in dating and relationships, and let beta men be themselves.

7: The "He Must Be a Compatible Personality Type" Story

As an alpha woman, if one of your mate selection criterions is to find a man with the same or a similar Myers-Briggs Personality Type as you, for example, and you are not having any luck, it's because opposite energies (brain types) attract. And having different brain types causes people to have different personality types.

According to Katya Varbanova,[32] an expert on the cognitive functions of different types of men and women, alpha women are typically masculine personality types:

ENTJ or INTJ
ESTP or ISTP
ENFJ or INFJ
ESFP or ISFP

Beta men are typically feminine personality types:

ENTP or INTP
ENFP or INFP
ESFJ or ISFJ
ESTJ or ISTJ

Katya also says most alpha women will *never* attract the same personality type because, "They need a feminine dude." And that, "You should never date yourself anyway."

The same is likely true for other personality type tests, such as the DISC or Strength Finder. The most commonly understood personality types are Type A and Type B.

> **Type A Personality:** More competitive, ambitious, highly organized, often obsessive about time management, and impatient.

> **Type B Personality:** Less competitive, ambitious in different ways, often disorganized, go-with-the-flow, and a little more patient.

As a general rule, Type A attracts Type B, regardless of gender (and sexual orientation). Extremely Type A attracts extremely Type B.

As long as an alpha woman continues to *believe* she deserves a man who's just like her, and bases dating decisions on a personality test versus complementary traits, she will not open herself up to the type of man who would be better suited to her. Please don't make the same mistake.

Astrological Signs: No matter which sign is supposedly your perfect match, as an alpha-dominant woman, you are *going to* attract a beta-dominant man who will likely be very different than you. My advice is to stop looking for your "twin flame." Select your highly desirable guy and start dating, learn all about each other, and adapt as you go.

8: The "He Must Match My Level of Orderliness" Story

Some alpha women state they'd never date a man who's messy, or who isn't as neat and tidy as they are. As an alpha woman, you are much more likely to be better organized than the typical beta man because your personal space—such as your office desk, your vehicle or your home—reflects *how your brain processes information.*

Your brain, the "male brain," compartmentalizes the pieces of your life into individual boxes. As a general rule, the boxes are not supposed to "touch each other." As a result, it may be much easier for you to keep things tidier, more organized, and in sequential order—including your career life, your social life, and your dating life. From your perspective, everything in your home likely has a distinct place where it belongs—spices may be alphabetized in the pantry, dishes loaded a certain way in the dishwasher, books categorized by subject matter in the bookshelf, shoes and clothes organized by color and season, and so on. Again, this is how the "male brain" is structured.

The beta man's brain, the "female brain," has no such compartmentalization mechanism. There's a big difference between knowing where things belong and actually being able to keep them that way. This is why they may have dishes stacked up in the sink and one or two on the coffee table; clothes in the closet and others scattered across the floor, the couch, or the bed; books, paperwork, and bills spread from the kitchen to an office desk and beyond; and so on. As a general rule, since there are no boxes—everything is connected to everything—it can make keeping things tidy, organized, and in sequential order much more challenging—including their career, their social calendar, and their dating life.

While that might be frustrating to some, having a predominantly "female brain" can be an advantage in many areas of life, such as empathizing with others, multi-tasking, rich verbal communication, retrieving information from long-term memory, and connecting seemingly unrelated insights from totally different fields. As Dr. Brizendine said, "It is my hope that the female brain will be seen and understood as the finely tuned and talented instrument that is actually is."[33] Still, almost all strengths come with drawbacks, like not being able to keep one's home or office neat and organized. There are no "perfect" people.

Undoubtedly, some men are bigger slobs than others. But just know his personal space is a reflection of how his brain processes information, not necessarily a conscious choice to be lazy, messy, or disorganized. Of course, having standards of orderliness is fine, and this will be one area where you and your man likely will need to compromise. You may need to relax your rules and be okay with dishes in the sink sometimes, and he will need to be more aware and clean up after himself.

9: The "He Must Be Able to Keep Up with Me" Story

If you are an extremely or mostly alpha-dominant woman, particularly in your mid-thirties and beyond, and you are having a hard time finding a mostly beta man who's equally as busy, active, and physically fit as you, know this: Many extremely or mostly alpha women (and men) have far more physical energy and stamina than everyone else—very likely due to innate hormonal differences, such as the "testosterone surge" in utero that Dr. Brizendine says turns the "female brain" into a "male brain."

Testosterone is closely associated with aggression, building strength and muscle, a higher sex drive, and a go-go-go lifestyle—"alpha-like" traits. Estrogen and oxytocin are known to manifest in desires such as relaxing, cuddling, nurturing, helping, and serving others—"beta-like" traits. It seems logical to me that extremely or mostly beta-dominant men (and women) may have higher relative levels of estrogen and oxytocin (or dopamine), or simply lower relative levels of testosterone—innately, or due to some other anomaly.

Whatever the case may be, higher alphas, having more physical energy, can lead to a lot more time running, working out, or some other form of physical fitness—plus shorter recovery times due to a higher pain tolerance and lower levels of muscle soreness. As a result, many have more lean muscle, lower body fat, a higher metabolism, and a *lot* more energy than many beta and balanced men (and women). So, if you are a mostly alpha woman, and you're having a difficult time finding an "equal opposite" man who can keep up with you in these ways, you will likely need to realign your mate selection criterion accordingly.

Remember, the primary purpose of polar attraction is vibrational and/or hormonal balance—meaning the beta man will help you feel more *energetically feminine,* and you will help him feel more *energetically masculine.* And together, you are the whole enchilada.

Female Body Image Tip

If you are not overly active, or you have a more "normal" body shape, or are more "curvy," do *not* compare yourself to "super alpha women" (if you do) because they almost certainly have innate genetic advantages. But you may be able to look more like them (if you desire to) if you follow a similar nutrition and exercise routine.

Regardless, many beta men work hard to eat right and stay in pretty good shape by *their* standards, or are more naturally trim. If you are into yoga, find a man who's open to trying yoga with you. If you are a triathlete and he's not, he might love to watch you race and root you on to victory. If you are more of a homebody and don't care about any of this, find a guy who simply loves you for you. Beauty comes in all shapes and sizes, and different men (and women) have different preferences.

The Big Takeaway

Taking all of this into consideration, you might want to consider tweaking a few of your socially programmed "stories" and personal preferences, and start looking for a very special beta man who *actually* commonly exists.

I'm not asking you to settle. In fact, I'm asking you to do the opposite—to actively realign your mate selection, courtship, and financial expectations with the beta man's reality today. Opposites attract and the primary purpose of polar attraction is energetic balance.

Truth

Men have "stories" about how *you* are "supposed" to be too, based on what *they* were taught to believe and their own personal assumptions. For example, you "should be" between 5'0' and 5'8" and weigh 115 to 130 pounds; be more in touch with your feelings and eager to share them; be more *energetically* feminine (playful, light-hearted, and girly); more sensitive and empathetic of their feelings; less of a ballbuster; not so bossy.

Their "stories" and expectations of alpha-dominant (and balanced) women *also* need revisions. You can help make that happen by encouraging them to read this book.

Note: Since dating is a team activity, it's their *New Dating Playbook*, too.

Again, I've been reading and studying "chick" books, magazines, and movies since high school, in an effort to get *both* perspectives. It's not unmanly, it's crafty and smart.

How Tweaking Your "Stories" Can Set You Up for Dating Success

The following examples demonstrate common pairing mistakes many alpha women make when attempting to date according to their social programming-influenced stories. See if you can identify with any of their dating frustrations and confusion. Then see how they turned it around.

Example 1

Ashley, a schoolteacher in her late twenties, said she wanted a kind and compassionate man who loves helping others and wants to have kids. She was correctly searching for a complementary beta man. But Ashley rarely got asked out and didn't understand why men weren't approaching her.

When she started using her alpha-dominant qualities in her dating life, by approaching men and introducing herself instead of waiting for beta men to come to her, she met a great guy who volunteered with kids at their church. They are now married and expecting their first child.

Example 2

Sheila is a thirty-nine-year-old successful attorney who had never been married, and desperately wanted to have her own children. She was active on three popular dating apps and got more than her fair share of attention. But no matter where she looked, she couldn't find a man who had the best qualities of both an alpha man and a beta man—for example, a naturally assertive, take-charge type who makes at least six figures; *and* a chivalrous, romantic, sweet and thoughtful man with emotional depth. She was unknowingly choosing to stay single, and might never have gotten married and had her own children, all because of the incongruent social programming and personal assumptions she never thought to second-guess.

Fortunately, she learned some of these key principles and began dating according to the *New Dating Playbook* rules. In a matter of months, she attracted a quality man three years younger than her. They are now engaged, and plan to marry and have a baby as soon as possible.

Example 3

Michelle is a forty-seven-year-old single mom, an elite medical sales rep, and a part-time fitness model. She spends her free time enjoying luxury travel, playing golf, lifting weights, and riding horses.

Her online dating profile said she was looking for her "active other half"—a man who's just like her. She also considered it very important for the men she dated to make at least as much money as her—$300,000 a year. Despite being a remarkably attractive woman with tons to offer a great beta man, she'd been single for years and couldn't figure out what was going on.

When she learned she's an extremely alpha-dominant woman, how the Law of Polarity works, and the innate differences between her and extremely beta-dominant men, she *wasn't* pleased. But eventually she accepted reality and texted a handful of her favorite previous dates—men who made less money than her, and were a little less active, but enjoyed doing similar activities.

Michelle is now in a loving relationship with a fine beta man, and she knows exactly what to do differently to keep their relationship healthy and strong. She doesn't know if she wants to get married again, but she's enjoying the ride.

Alpha Women Have Risen

According to Pew Research Center analysis from the U.S. Census Bureau in 2013, "40% of all households with children under the age of 18 include mothers who are either the sole or primary source of income for the family." It was 11% in 1960. That 40% statistic is seven years old and the numbers are likely even greater now. When the next census data is released, I fully expect women—likely alpha women, in particular—to be *dominating* men in almost every economic category, considering today:[34]

- More girls than boys graduate from high school.[35]
- Considerably more women go to and graduate from college.[36]
- Women decisively outnumber men in graduate school.
- Women now earn the majority of doctoral degrees.[37]
- Women make up the majority of new enrollees in law and medical schools.
- Single women buy their own homes at more than twice the rate of single men.[38]
- The majority of managers are now women.
- On average, women are scoring higher on IQ tests than men.

In summary, women are kicking men's butts.

According to Tucker Carlson from Fox News, "Whenever gender differences come up in public debates, the so-called wage gap dominates the conversation. 'A woman makes 77 cents for every dollar a man makes.' That's the statistic you'll hear. But that number compares all American men to all American women across all professions. No legitimate social scientist would consider that a valid measure. The number is both meaningless and intentionally misleading. Once you compare men and women with similar experience working the same hours in similar jobs for the same period of time—and that's the only way you can measure it—the gap all but disappears. In fact, it may invert. One study using census data found that single women in their 20s living in metropolitan areas now earn 8% more on average than their male counterparts."[39]

The gender pay gap claim has been debunked over and over again. And not only that, it seems the old statistics are still being promoted at the highest level to keep women feeling stuck and frustrated. According to a 2016 *Forbes* article by Karin Agness Lips, "The White House and others who promote the myth are manipulating statistics in a way to convince women that they are the victims of systemic societal discrimination, and, therefore, stand to benefit from further government action."[40]

According to Dr. Sonya Rhodes, "In 147 out of 150 of the biggest cities in the United States, unmarried, childless women under thirty earn 8 percent to 15 percent more than their male peers."[41] And the trend is likely to continue. In 2015, researchers at the University of Missouri and the University of Glasgow in Glasgow, Scotland, used international data to conclude, "Girls outperform boys in educational achievement in 70 percent of the countries they studied—regardless of the level of gender, political, economic or social equality."[42]

Here's an even more recent statistic you might have heard. According to a 2017 report by Sheryl Sandberg and the McKinsey Company, "Only 10% of senior executives are women."[43] I agree that's far from ideal. But at huge corporations in which men have likely been in power for decades, they are not likely to step down just to make room for more women. If you were in their position, would you give up your job just so a man could have it?

Note: Look for these stats to drastically change in women's favor in the coming years!

Lastly, if most men still make more money than most women, why are so many financially successful (or stable), single women complaining that they can't find a man they like who makes more money than they do? (Do an online search for "women not marrying because of men".)

Note: I know tons of mostly alpha women who make three-to-five times as much money as the mostly beta men they attract. Now *there's* a gender wage gap statistic I'd love to see.

In summary, the matriarchy now has a foothold and is gathering momentum. Regardless of what you believe about which gender currently makes the most, it's much more balanced than ever before.

Note: If you are big on impeccable Ph.D. research, and want *tons* more evidence that women are rising and men—likely beta men, in particular—are falling in nearly every socioeconomic category, I recommend the book, *The Boy Crisis: Why Our Boys Are Struggling and What We Can Do About It*, by Warren Farrell, Ph.D., and John Gray, Ph.D., author of *Men Are from Mars, Women Are from Venus*. (In my opinion, Dr. Farrell and Dr. Gray are both "from Venus.")

> **Challenge:** Find and watch the three-minute YouTube video titled, "Jordan Peterson Completely Destroys Feminist Narrative." If you hate Jordan Peterson (very likely mostly beta) and would prefer a *woman's* perspective, watch the TEDx YouTube video titled, "Meeting the Enemy: A Feminist Comes to Terms with the Men's Rights Movement," by Cassie Jaye (very likely mostly alpha).

The point I want to make here is that you cannot insist on tearing down the patriarchy (and succeed) and still date according to patriarchal beliefs. No matter who caused what, the equation just doesn't work. But because most women were taught that men *should* make more money than them in the dating world, simply because they are men, as women have risen, many alpha women's financial expectations for suitable beta male partners likely went *up,* instead of down—creating the conundrum that exists today.

Thankfully, a new style of teamwork will make the *new* dream work, too.

In light of these insights, I encourage you to embrace these new dating concepts as an alpha woman, and use your "superpowers" to lift beta men up and partner together for your mutual benefit.

Female Superheroes Are in Demand

"With great power comes great responsibility."

—The *Spiderman* Movie

If you are an extremely or mostly alpha-dominant woman, you were born with *genetically* superior "superpowers," such as:

- More physical energy, greater endurance, a relatively higher pain tolerance, and a longer life span.

- Greater orderliness, organizational skills, and self-control (more logical, less emotional).

- Countless business advantages like being more driven, assertive, independent, competitive, and often feeling more fulfilled by financial success and power.

Simply being born an alpha woman in the West in recent decades, *especially* one that the world views as particularly attractive, can also be a massive advantage in many areas of life—because women look up to you, men want to be with you, and males you don't even know will often go out of their way to cater to you. You also garner attention more quickly than most men, and are likely more persuasive in various ways, such as getting out of speeding tickets more easily, and negotiating better deals on everything from vehicles to new homes. Women also benefit from sexist freebies like "ladies' night" specials at bars and nightclubs, whereas men usually have to pay.

In summary, you have "alpha woman privilege."

Note: Yes, men enjoy a few privileges today, too, but nowhere near as many as ever before. And yes, historically, *some* men have treated women like second-class citizens, or worse. But most single men today *aren't* those men. All they've ever known is what it's like to be a man in *this* day and age.

As we all know, our revered fictional heroes don't save other heroes, because the gifted don't need to be saved. Superheroes partner with people who *don't* have their extraordinary gifts.

Again, I understand the real-world desire to partner with a man with the same level of strengths that you possess. But as we've discussed, that's not how polar attraction works. Opposites attract because being with a partner with complementary strengths makes you whole, and challenges you to learn and grow—both individually and as a couple.

The best movies have a kick-ass leading actor and a complementary supporting actor. Your path to a blockbuster love life could be the same.

So, remember Alpha Woman, with great power comes great responsibility.

Note: If you are not an extremely or mostly alpha woman, or these advantages do not describe you, you have other "superpowers."

We all do. I encourage you to use them to love and serve yourself and others.

Dee Devlin: A Modern-Day Superhero

Have you ever heard of a woman named Dee Devlin? She's not well known on her own. But she should be because her love story with her long-time boyfriend—sports celebrity, UFC Champion, and serial entrepreneur, Conor McGregor—is one for the ages.

If you're not familiar with McGregor, he's the trash-talking mixed martial arts champion from Ireland who crossed over into boxing to fight the undefeated world boxing champion, Floyd Mayweather, in the summer of 2017. He lost that fight. But according to ESPN,[44] McGregor was paid $30 million.

As of 2019, according to Celebrity Net Worth,[45] McGregor's net worth is approximately $110 million. But guess how much he was worth when he met his eventual long-term girlfriend, Dee Devlin? Essentially *nothing*.

When they met in a Dublin nightclub in 2008, McGregor was collecting weekly $215 unemployment checks—that's $10,750 a year.[46] But Dee saw something in him and he made her laugh. The two started dating. She drove him to and from the gym to train. She had a great job at the time, was the breadwinner for the couple, and worked extra hard to buy him nutritious food and everything he needed to become a better fighter.

But most importantly, she *believed* in him.

In McGregor's own words, **"She saved my life."**

In 2015, McGregor told *MMA Fighting*, "My girlfriend has been there since the start. She has helped me throughout this career. If it wasn't for her, I probably wouldn't be where I am today." He added, "My girlfriend worked very hard throughout the years and stuck by me when I had essentially absolutely nothing. I only had a dream that I was telling her.[47]

"For me to be able to take her out of work, give her everything she's ever wanted, and to travel the world with her fills me with pride. It keeps me going. We've been together a long time. She's been through it all with me."[48]

Now there's a woman who *deserves* to be treated like a queen.

There's a popular Internet meme that says, "Most women want a man who's already successful. A strong woman will be part of his struggle, survive it, succeed together, and build an empire." That's exactly what Dee Devlin did for Conor McGregor. Had she not stepped in and joined him during his struggle, he might still be unemployed, or worse. Instead they're worth roughly $110 million, and he continues to be her loyal, loving man.

Recently, I shared this popular meme on my Instagram page. I received the following comment from an extremely alpha-dominant single woman follower: "Most of my lady friends have built their own empire, and hope that a man is secure in his. Then they come together to be even more powerful. There shouldn't be any expectation of helping or pouring themselves into another, right?"

I replied, "Do your girlfriends want transactional love or transformational love? If they don't want to help or pour themselves into their partner, what kind of a relationship are they looking for?"

Many financially successful (or financially focused) women I've talked to, who are usually extremely or mostly alpha-dominant women, seem to be longing for transactional love—an even trade. *You give me this and I'll give you that. Or you have your empire and I have mine, and together we will rule the world.* **This *isn't* love.**

Note: I extend this alpha woman IG follower and her girlfriends kindness and compassion because they likely have limited knowledge about how polar attraction works, or what it's like to be an extremely or mostly beta man in this day and age. As Sheryl Sandberg said, "We cannot change what we are not aware of, and once we are aware, we cannot help but change."

Whether a man makes more than you, less than you, or about the same, joining forces and building a fabulous life together is a winning formula for success and life-long loyalty. Most beta men's potential for greatness will also increase with a woman like you on his team, and the same will likely be true for you. So, imagine the possibilities you two could create together. And remember, it's not where you start that matters most, but where you two finish as a *unit*.

> "Change your story, change your life. Divorce the story of limitation, and marry the story of truth and everything changes."
>
> —TONY ROBBINS

Ideally, you should now be ready to consider changing some of your internal stories to align with the Law of Polarity. This will play a major success in mate selection, countless dating dynamics we have yet to discuss, various lifestyle considerations, and more.

Again, I absolutely empathize with the desire to find a man who has the best qualities of both energy types. But it's far better to know the truth and make informed dating decisions, than to continue looking for a man who very likely does not exist—an alpha man with whom you share a desirable polar attraction and overall compatibility, or a beta man who fits all of your alpha man "stories."

I encourage you to follow Dee's lead and look for a hidden jewel of man you can invest in, share your innate gifts with, and build a true partnership. Whether you two start a successful business together someday or not, you'll have built something money can't buy—true love.

Challenge: If you want to see another example of what being a real-life superhero looks like (and an incredible example of what true love looks like), watch the YouTube video, "Wife helps her navy seal husband to recover after car accident." I guarantee you this scenario *wasn't* part of her original "story." But she went above and beyond to help her husband recover. (She's very likely mostly alpha, too.)

Chapter 6

THE NEW DATING PLAYBOOK FOR BADASS WOMEN

"Get up, right now. Rise up from where you've been, scrub away the tears and the pain of yesterday, and start again . . . Girl, wash your face!"

—RACHEL HOLLIS, *GIRL, WASH YOUR FACE*

Many women (and men) treat the initial dating process like it's a beautiful box that is *already* full of the things they long for, like companionship, intimacy, and security. The truth is when you first start talking to a guy, the potential for an epic relationship is like an empty box. You must fill the box *before* you try to take things out, by investing in each other and both being selfless and loving. If you take the opposite approach and are primarily *self-seeking* during your initial conversations and dates, you will likely continue to struggle with dating and relationships *until* you adopt a "fill the box first" mentality and focus on being an excellent teammate.

This *New Dating Playbook* will empower you to be the best companion a man has ever met, which will naturally lead to a soul-stirring love life faster and easier. As an alpha woman, it's up to you set the pace.

Take the Lead or Lead a Man to Lead You

As a strong, independent, ambitious, and/or financially successful woman, you are in the driver's seat. You are fully capable of taking the lead and making your relationship dreams a reality, and it will be crucial for you to do so. But you might still want to be led some, too.

To help you bridge this gap with the beta men you date, I created a technique I call "Lead a man to lead you." In many instances, you will be the primary leader, a co-leader if you prefer, and you will communicate with a man in ways that will empower him to lead you how you want him to—a win-win. Strong beta men don't want you to take the lead entirely; they simply want you to *guide* them to some degree. You will discover many different ways to "lead a man to lead you" in the remaining chapters. But first, let's discuss the three laws of this *New Dating Playbook*.

The 3 Laws of This New Dating Playbook

This *New Dating Playbook* is founded on three psychology-based laws of human nature. As you apply these principles, you will also distinguish yourself in meaningful ways, making you a far more appealing first date, girlfriend, and potential lifelong mate.

1. The Law of Polarity

As an alpha-dominant woman, you are the more natural leader. Remember, masculine energy—however much you have—wants to hunt, chase, and pursue. Feminine energy wants to be sought after and pursued. You may also want to be needed, and being the leader automatically makes you needed and valuable. Beta men want to be wanted, and being pursued by you automatically makes them feel satisfied in that regard. You've both undoubtedly been indoctrinated to believe the opposite. But the essence of your respective core desires is still present, and it always will be. Therefore, the natural order of events in your dating life should be for you to act initially and then see how the men react to you. This is the most powerful position to be in because it gives you a tremendous amount of personal power, as you can evaluate if the men respond how you want them to.

2. The Law of Reciprocity

The Law of Reciprocity is based on the Vedic principle that every action has an equal and opposite reaction. It states that most people will reciprocate in like fashion to how they are treated, also known as mirroring. If you begin a conversation with a man in a weak way, he will typically mirror your weakness—a lose-lose. For example, if you message a guy, "Hi, how's your week going?" He will likely respond with, "Great, how's your week going?" Boring. (You will discover many ways to start strong in the remaining chapters.) The Law of Reciprocity is extremely important to remember, because as the initiator, you should be initiating and setting the tone for most of your dating interactions, especially very early in the relationship. As you will see, when you start strong, most men will mirror your strength—a win-win. The Law of Reciprocity also applies to taking turns planning and paying for dates.

3. The Law of Differentiation

Dating is competitive. You are constantly being compared to other single women, the same way you compare and contrast different men. Some men might assume you're a woman who treats men *very poorly* by using them for free drinks, dinners, or entertainment, with no intention of ever reciprocating in any manner. Therefore, it's important to differentiate yourself in a *desirable* way from your true competition—other alpha women. Believe it or not, being a loving and generous dater can actually cause a man to see you as even more physically attractive than he initially thought. For example, if you are flirtatious and fun, and you buy the first or second round of drinks, his *perception* of you (and your inner and outer beauty) can easily go from an eight to a ten. That being said, if you are perceived as acting entitled, sexist, and selfish, his opinion of you can go from a ten to a two just as quickly—and the same is most likely true for you based on how a man treats you.

Successful dating is 80% psychology and 20% execution. Adopt these three laws of human nature—the Law of Polarity, the Law of Reciprocity, and the Law of Differentiation—for alpha women and beta men, and you will get far better and faster results.

The Best Teams Make the Best Couples

True happiness and inner fulfillment are what bring peace, love, and joy to your soul. And being a successful team *as a couple* is the best way to make this happen. To accomplish this, your beta man needs to feel that his innate gifts and talents are valued, and that there's no need for you two to compete because you're in the same band.

The following chart is meant to show examples of how you and your future man are going to make an excellent team by playing different "roles" that clearly *complement* each other. And *together* you'll be the total package.

There's nothing for you to circle because this is not a quiz. Instead, your man and you will create your *own* version of this chart based on your respective strengths and weaknesses, life goals as a couple, and other attributes.

Alpha Woman +	Beta Man =	Co-Champions
Appearance + Social Life Attractive, striking, confident, stage presence, the prize	**Appearance + Social Life** Stand-up guy, loves to show you off, supportive	**Appearance + Social Life** Super team, awesome couple, allows you to set the pace
Business/Career Go-getter, organized, planner, hard worker, results driven, big sales, close the deal	**Business/Career** Creative, visionary, collaborator, purpose driven, wants buyer to be satisfied	**Business/Career** Winning team; the best businesses must sell and deliver on their promises
Lovers Often prefer to be pleased; may be more of a receiver than a giver	**Lovers** Often prefers to please; may be more of a giver than a receiver	**Lovers** A win-win, but strive to achieve balance for your mutual benefit

The Best Dating Philosophy

When it comes to success with men and dating, *a team-based men-tality* is the only way to win. Therefore, the best dating philosophy is to provide as much value as possible for your potential partner—the men you meet, talk to, and date—instead of sitting back and waiting for them to provide value first.

Take back your personal power and focus on demonstrating your own ability to meet and exceed their needs, wants, and desires. I recommend doing so at the very beginning of a new relationship, such as messaging a man online or meeting him in person for the first time, because you only get one chance to make a great first impression. Then continue to focus on adding value throughout every stage of a successful relationship, while also making sure he's doing his best to reciprocate, because successful relationships are a two-way street. **Just remember, his best will be based on his natural strengths, not yours. And the reverse will be true for you.**

Throw away any old beliefs you have that cause you to believe it's the man's job to do just about everything first, and start being the real you—the person you are when you're attempting to make a new friend, or to woo a new client and earn their business.

- Stop looking for your equal and start looking for a man who complements you.

- Stop waiting for beta men to do everything first and take back your personal power by being more proactive in your search for true love.

- Stop pretending to be a passive woman and be the real you.

OLD DATING PLAYBOOK (As an alpha woman)	NEW DATING PLAYBOOK (As an alpha woman)
Mistruths & Misunderstandings	Truth & Love
Reactive	Proactive
"That's *his* job." (Fake You)	"I got this!" (Real You)
Adversarial Relationship	Partnership
One-sided	Equality
Win-Lose	Win-Win

5 Qualities Beta Men Desire in a Woman

Different men desire different things in a woman at different times for different reasons, and the same is true for you. So, you will want to read through the following information with the understanding that there is a degree of stereotyping here. Remember, we are all *individuals*.

1. Visual Attractiveness

Most men are visually oriented creatures. You will feel and look your best when you live an active, healthy lifestyle. Beta men will, too. Just remember they don't always have the same physical energy levels. Ideally you both love each other for what's on the inside more than the outside. But maintaining your beauty and sexiness is important, too.

2. Vulnerable Communication

Many beta men crave vulnerable communication. There's no right or wrong answer here. They simply want to know what's going on within your beautiful mind. What do you think about? What do you want? What scares you? What pleases you? Remember, beta men see the world through the lens of good versus bad, whereas you may see the world through the lens of strong versus weak. You might view vulnerability as being weak. But in the beta man's world, vulnerable communication is often an essential component. Not showing weakness is a sign of weakness, not strength, because it takes a strong person to be vulnerable and transparent.

3. Win His Heart

Beta men might not tell you this, but they want you to win their heart, too. The best way to accomplish this is by doing the little things many people take for granted, like writing thoughtful notes on yellow stickies and hiding them in places you know he'll find, or buying him creative gifts that are unique to him. Again, there is no right or wrong answer. It's the thought and your effort that matter most.

In chapter 9, I will present a five-step formula you can use to generate an endless supply of one-of-a-kind ways to show a man that you like him, love him, or want him.

4. The 4 Most Powerful Words You Can Say to a Man

The four most powerful words you could ever say to a beta man are **"I believe in you."** This is extremely important to say *out loud* to a man you're fighting for, or a man you really want to romance you. It's not a phrase to be taken lightly or thrown around meaninglessly. If you *do* mean it, you don't have to wait until you're in a serious relationship. Knowing you are his biggest cheerleader will make him want to do his best for you—*his* primary motivation.

Again, many beta men are nowhere near as fearless or confident as you may be, even if they pretend to be. Many want to play the gender role society has been telling them they're "supposed to" play for you—that of a mighty warrior who will love, serve, and protect you. But many men don't believe they have what it takes to be successful, particularly when it comes to providing for you financially. (Note: Some beta men are great providers, but aren't great daters.)

No matter how hard they try, they're never going to be a natural-born alpha like you, the same way you're never going to be just like them. But hearing you say, "I believe in you," should give them a boost in confidence and self-belief. You'll need to say this repeatedly (but not randomly) because most men like repetition, and will likely desire to be continuously aware that you believe in him, and that you're with him all the way. For example, when he's having a tough time at work, or making an effort to eat healthier to lose weight or get in better shape, your verbally expressed confidence in him, and ongoing encouragement, will do wonders for his self-confidence—a win-win.

5. A Triple Threat Beta Men Can't Resist

Strong beta men want a woman who knows when, where, and how to balance being a lady, a romantic, and a "naughty girl." For example, he wants you to be a lady or a respectable woman around his parents and at dinner parties. This includes having good manners, speaking eloquently, and being polite and complimentary of him and your relationship. Other times he wants you to listen and learn about his needs, wants, and desires. Then surprise him with sweet, thoughtful, and romantic gestures that show him how you feel about him. This includes everything from birthday gifts to wearing suggestive outfits and being playful, flirtatious, affectionate, and loving. In the bedroom, mix it up. Maybe one week you're more lady-like; the next week you're a romantic; and the following week you're in the mood for something a little more sultry and spontaneous. This might involve you two playing "teacher" and "student" in "detention," but it could also be much simpler—such as a kitchen quickie, or an unplanned and uninhibited display of ravenous affection.

Aim to be a lady, a romantic, and a "bad girl" at different times and in different places. For example, you might act like a lady and a romantic when having dinner with your man at a nice restaurant. But later whisper something "inappropriate" in his ear, or text him while you're using the ladies' room. The keys to this formula are timing, discretion, and balance.

> The Lady = A woman he respects.
> The Romantic = A woman he loves.
> The Bad Girl = A woman he lusts for.

This formula might seem overly simplistic, but you'd be amazed how many women (and men) drop the ball when it comes to playing *all three* of these roles. For example, a woman might be the most adventurous lover he's ever been with. But if she curses like a sailor at inappropriate times, she's missing the lady part of the equation, or at least has room for improvement.

Note: "Acting ladylike" will be different for different women. In some cases, it may mean saying "please" and "thank you." In others, it may mean controlling the volume of her voice when she talks. Being ladylike doesn't have one definition. As an adult, you know what "acting ladylike" means for you. Be yourself but remember your audience at any given moment.

Here's another example: A woman commands her man's respect, and has no problem "misbehaving" when appropriate. But if she doesn't listen to her man and reciprocate with creative, thoughtful, or romantic gestures, she's missing the romantic part of the equation. Most women believe it's the man's job to be romantic, but relationships are a two-way street. Therefore, it's your assignment, too.

Lastly, maybe she's a lady in public and writes him the sweetest love letters. But in the bedroom, she's shy and reserved, or holds back more than he'd prefer. She most likely has a saucy side in there somewhere, but she won't throw caution to the wind and show him, no matter how many times he asks her to. She might believe showing her man that side of her would make him not want her anymore. In reality, it would only make him want her more.

Note: If you are waiting for marriage to have sex, your man still wants to know that once you are married, you'll have a naughty side, too. Just because you aren't having sex doesn't mean you aren't kissing or getting handsy, so show him you think he's bootylicious by grabbing his butt or having a steamy make out session. You could also tell him you have a wild side or write him a letter and show him the kinds of thoughts you're capable of thinking, and what you're looking forward to acting out with him on your honeymoon.

Again, strive to be a lady, a romantic, and a "naughty girl" at different times and in different places. Experiment and see what works for the two of you, and what doesn't. Do more of what brings success and have fun.

How to Find the Guy for You

Finding a great man requires *actively* looking for him. That means being more aware of your surroundings everywhere you go, and having the confidence to initiate a conversation and introduce yourself when an opportunity presents itself, as opposed to sitting back and hoping a beta man approaches you.

There's no right or wrong place to meet a man. You could be reading a book at your local coffee shop, meeting your girlfriends for happy hour, traveling for business, working out at the gym, or even grocery shopping. So, keep your eyes open everywhere you go. Another option is to look for men who enjoy doing similar things that you are doing. If you're into spirituality and meditation, join a yoga studio. If your faith is important to you and you're looking for a man with similar beliefs, join a church and get involved, go on a mission trip, or volunteer for a local charity. If you love playing golf or tennis, you can frequent a club or facilities. Do what you love to do, or go where you think the kind of men you want to meet also go. It's pretty straightforward.

Next, you've got to get his attention, actually meet him, and create some chemistry. Notice I said *create*. That's an action, meaning you are mutually responsible for making this happen. As you will see, there are many ways to go about this.

How will you know if a guy is interested in you? The truth is you don't need to know for sure. If you're interested in him, you have every right to go over and try to make a great first impression. Don't feel like you have to get a man's approval prior to approaching him. But here are a few ways to know if a man is interested in you, so you can make your move and let him know you're interested, too.

Indicators of Interest

Eye Contact

First and foremost, beta men choose alpha women primarily with their eyes. If you notice a man checking you out repeatedly, or if you two make strong eye contact—like two magnets—he's almost certainly interested in meeting you. Maybe one or both of you smile. He's actually more likely to smile and you're more likely to not show much emotion—the opposite of how alpha men and beta women generally respond to eye contact for the first time.

The *more* attractive he finds you, however, the *less* likely he will be to come over and talk to you, especially if you are with friends and you don't give him a clear "greenlight" to approach you. But there's a good chance he won't be able to take his eyes off of you. It's simply his natural way of expressing admiration. Remember, you were born to pursue, whereas he was born to attract and be pursued.

Nervousness

A beta man will often display a nervous, fear-based emotion when he is attracted to an alpha woman. If a guy acts a little apprehensive around you, anxious or insecure, or he's more quiet and reserved acting than he might normally be, he probably likes you. I imagine when you develop a crush on a man and think about trying to talk to him, you get a little nervous too, and might crack a few jokes to break the ice, or act a little weird because you're out of your comfort zone.

You've been taught to desire a strong, overly confident man. But for a beta man, being somewhat apprehensive around you and not sure what to say or do next is *actually* a sign of awe, wonder, and respect. If you're seeking a man who will take you seriously and treat you like fine gold, you should want him to be a bit daunted in your presence. A man who's not mesmerized by you, or doesn't respect you, is the type of man who's most likely to play with your heart and stomp on it after he gets what he wants.

If a man acts a little peculiar around you—shows interest with his eyes or goes out of his way to say hello whenever he sees you—he most certainly likes you. He's simply not sure what to do next because he prefers to react. That's the role he feels the most confident in.

Attention

Whether through a dating app, a social media platform, texting by phone, or in person, any form of focused attention is an indicator of interest. That includes adding you as a friend on Facebook and liking at least one photo of yours; following you on Instagram; "randomly" crossing paths with you at the grocery store; or simply saying hello, complimenting you, and attempting to strike up a casual conversation.

Even if he seems like "just a friend" because he's never really flirted with you or asked you out, he could still see you as "more than a friend" potentially. Some men don't like having female friends they're not attracted to. Yes, that sounds terrible. And yes, there are exceptions. But for the most part, if a man is giving you any form of consistent attention, he probably is interested.

> "We have all been there: we see that gorgeous person across the room, and we want to go and speak to them so badly. However, the 'rules' of society mean we usually don't end up doing it, despite our friends' best efforts to convince us to. Time for a change. Be empowered and say hi! It's proven that people really like it when you take initiative."
>
> —WHITNEY WOLFE HERD

If a man gives you one of these signs, and you are interested in getting to know him, your best bet is to engage and talk to him, or give him a reason to talk to you. If you don't engage, he will probably assume you aren't interested. If *he* doesn't engage, it usually means he wants to but isn't sure how to proceed, and doesn't want to make you uncomfortable or get rejected.

Approaching Men: Online or in Person

"Stop wearing your wishbone where your backbone ought to be."

—ELIZABETH GILBERT

When you pick up on these cues—prolonged eye contact, nervousness, and focused attention—get ready to make your move. Pretend he's a client or a potential new friend and go talk to him. Ask him about himself and his interests. Compliment him. Show him you're interested. Maybe touch him on the arm or the shoulder. Life begins at the end of your comfort zone, so leave it more often and you'll be much more successful in life and love. Quit waiting to be picked and choose a man for yourself, or welcome a man who selects you.

If the idea of approaching a man makes you think, *Won't that make me look desperate?* That's simply a false interpretation. Does approaching a client or striking up a conversation with a stranger make you desperate? Of course not. That makes you ambitious and proactive. You get to choose the story you tell yourself, so change your story and change your love life.

Adopt the mantra: "If it is to be, it's up to me."[49]

How to Make a Great First Impression

"Be weird. Be random. Be who you are.
Because you never know who would love the person you hide."

—C.S. LEWIS

In the first episode of *The Bachelor* each season, the lucky guy stands outside of the mansion. Limousines full of beautiful women pull up one at a time, and each bachelorette has one chance to make an unforgettable first impression. Some wear creative outfits that show off their personality, profession, or passion. Others bring a special gift from the heart.

There is no right or wrong way. Use your imagination and be yourself. If you are feisty, be feisty. If you are flirty, be flirty. If you are thoughtful, be thoughtful. If you are nervous, admit you are nervous. If you're worried about coming across as anxious or insecure, don't fret about it. Being a little anxious or insecure can actually work in your favor because it demonstrates bravery, authenticity, and shows you care. If you are normally somewhat boring, leave your comfort zone and be anything but boring.

Whether you've made eye contact from afar or not, pump yourself up mentally, like you would just before running a race or making a big presentation at work. Take a deep breath, smile, and walk over and say hello to him. Smile; be confident; be vulnerable; be flirtatious; be human.

"Vulnerability sounds like truth and feels like courage. Truth and courage aren't always comfortable, but they're never weakness."

—BRENÉ BROWN

Most beta men haven't been approached more than a few times in their entire lives, if ever, so the mere act of approaching him and saying hello should make him feel good about himself, and put you in a great light, too. Who knows? Just saying hello and being flirtatious could be enough to persuade him to take the lead and start pursuing you.

Before I get into *what* you might consider saying when you first approach him, please know that *how* you say it is important, too. Be upbeat, positive, and enthusiastic. Everyone has feel-good chemicals in the brain, like dopamine and serotonin, which spike even more when others greet us in appealing ways.

When you first interact with a man, you will want to make him feel alive! Whatever you say, do it in a way that aims to wake him up from his normal, everyday life, and show him that you are the adventure he seeks. Sell him on the dream of being saved from a life of monotony and presented with the opportunity to battle for a woman who's equally committed to battling for him.

You undoubtedly already know what it feels like to be pursued. But to learn how a man wants you to make him feel, consider the following analogy. Imagine you're two years into a job that's going okay, when a recruiter contacts you unexpectedly about a promising new opportunity. Feels pretty cool, right? Maybe today is the day your life is going to change for the better and someone else is going to help you make it happen. Without even talking to you, they have a pretty good idea of what you're looking for next, too.

The recruiter begins to tell you about this amazing opportunity. *Tell me more,* you think to yourself. It's a terrific company, a place where everyone wants to work, because they're doing big things, impacting others, and they treat their employees like gold. *Wow, this does sound great*, you think. Before you even know the name of the company, you're emotionally intrigued and in a heightened state of mental curiosity. This is how men want you to make them feel, too.

If he is impressed with your delivery and also interested in getting to know you, he will light up on the inside and reciprocate with equal vigor and enthusiasm—skyrocketing your chances of hitting it off with each other and transitioning to exchanging numbers and concluding a successful first meeting.

14 Strong Conversation Starters

The best conversation starters are spontaneous, not canned or memorized one-liners. Approaching a guy may be a foreign concept to you, so here are a few *frameworks* to get you thinking about how to put your best foot forward and make a great first impression, whether meeting a man for the first time in person or messaging him online.

Note: All of these could be examples of leading a man to lead you. Due to the Law of Reciprocation, you being more leader-like empowers men to mirror your behavior and become more leader-like, too.

1. The Direct Approach

The direct approach is when you walk up to a guy without any real game plan, and say something simple and straightforward like: "Hi, I'm Elizabeth. That's a sharp tie you're wearing. Where are you headed tonight?" There are countless ways to vary this approach, depending on the man you're meeting or messaging online. But the three elements, regardless of the order in which you say them, are introduction, a compliment, and a question. This is a straightforward, simple approach that often yields surprisingly successful results.

2. The Awareness Approach

The awareness approach is similar to the direct approach, but more strategic. Before you talk to him or message him online, you're thinking about what to say based on the circumstances—what he's wearing or where the conversation is taking place. For example, if you're at the park and he's wearing gym clothes, you might ask him where he works out, whether he prefers machines or free weights, or if he thinks he could bench press you.

3. The Dale Carnegie "McDougal" Approach

In his bestselling book, *How to Win Friends and Influence People*, Carnegie says the secret to getting people to like you is to discover what *they* care about most, and then talk about that.

Ask a man what he's passionate about and you should have no trouble getting him to open up. However, if he says his passion is video games and you hate video games, this strategy could backfire. Therefore, I suggest you twist Carnegie's approach and start by asking questions about topics *you* are passionate about that you suspect he might be into, too. For example, if you play tennis and he has that "tennis player look"—athletic, thinner build, a little preppy—start there. If you enjoy shooting pool, ask him if he plays and if he's any good. Then maybe suggest a first date that encompasses your shared interest or hobby.

Identifying a common interest is the equivalent of hitting the jackpot, because a shared purpose or passion is one of the best ways to connect with a man.

4. The Wave Him Over to You Approach

If you make eye contact with a man in person—whether looking at each other from twenty yards or ten feet—and you want him to approach you, use your index finger or your whole hand and literally wave him over to you. Many beta men need or want your permission or approval to approach you. Considering you are dating in the "me too" era, which has many men even *more* hesitant to approach a woman, this is an excellent way to let a man know you're intrigued by him and want to get to know him.

5. The Bet

The bet is a continuation of the Dale Carnegie "McDougal" approach. Once you've found common ground, challenge him by saying something like: "I bet I can beat you at _____. Loser has to (buy drinks, wash the car, foot massage)."

Example 1: If you both play tennis, you might say, "Are you any good?" He says, "I can hold my own." Then you say, "I like your confidence. You're going to need it." You're both communicating you'd like to see each other for a tennis match date. Get his number or give him yours, then start texting and flirting between now and your first date. Your first date could be a tennis date, or you might suggest meeting for drinks and save your bet—whatever you two agree on—for your second or third date. Either way, you've upped the ante by suggesting a one-on-one competition.

Example 2: You meet a man at a sports bar and start talking about football. You ask if he knows which NFL quarterback has the most Super bowl rings, and he says it's Joe Montana. You think it's Tom Brady and you're confident you're right, so you suggest a bet— loser buys the next round of drinks, or loser has to write a short poem about how awesome the winner is and recite it the next time you two see each other. Once the terms of your bet are agreed upon, shake on it. Then pull out your smartphone and see who's right. Win or lose, you both win because you're having way more fun than if you two sat there and asked each other typical first date questions.

It can also set the stage for a fun future date before the present social situation has run its course.

6. The Story Approach

The story approach, also known as the current event approach, is when you ask a man if he knows about a recent topical event or shocking story from pop culture. For example, "Did you hear about the crazy lady who jumped the fence at The White House and tried to make out with one of the Secret Service agents?" It doesn't even have to have really happened. You can make it up. Once again, the goal is to break the normal routine of, "Hi, how are you? What's your name? What do you do for a living?" and engage a man in an emotional dialogue about something topical, unexpected, dramatic, or shocking. Your imagination will perk his.

7. The Joke Approach

Leading with a funny joke—even a corny "Dad" joke—can be a great way to break the ice and share a few laughs. Just make sure it won't be perceived as offensive. You can also aim to make him the butt of a joke by being creative and trying to get him to fall for something that isn't true—you made it up using the awareness approach.

For example, ten years ago, I bumped into a beautiful girl in a bar and noticed she was wearing one of those black and turquoise beaded yoga bracelets. (They are believed to bring one good karma, so I twisted the meaning.) I had a random thought and said to her, "You know that bracelet actually brings you bad karma, right?"

"Really?" she said, not quite sure if I was joking or not.

"Really," I replied—totally straight-faced.

"Nu-uh," she replied.

"Seriously," I stated, matter-of-factly.

A few minutes later, I let her in on my joke and gave her a hard time about how gullible she was, which she must've loved because we exchanged numbers and went on our first date a few days later. For our second date, we went skydiving, which was *her* idea and invitation.

Life is short, so have fun and live in the moment. Chemistry isn't logical. It's emotional, impulsive, and often rashly unpredictable.

8. The Show Approach

If a man *tells* you what kind of woman he's looking for—in person or in his online dating profile—it's fine to tell him you're that kind of woman. But it's far better to *show* him.

If a man says he loves to travel and you do, too, you could say, "Oh, I love traveling, too." Or you could show him pictures of a recent trip and tell him how he "would just love it there, we should go sometime!" Or drop an interesting tidbit of knowledge you picked up on a trip to a unique location, such as a recipe you learned about at a small bistro in Paris, or the crazy fans at a soccer game in Brazil.

Whether a man says he's into intellectual women, loves adventure, or enjoys witty banter, don't just tell him you're into that too. Show him the you that truly fits his ideal.

9. The Bold Compliment

The goal is to flatter him with a bold compliment, which will let him know you're interested and show him you are a confident woman. A bold compliment should feel a little risky. If you're not semi-scared to say it, it's not a bold enough compliment. This approach is a calculated risk, but the potential rewards are bigger, too.

It can also be a spontaneous reaction or revelation about yourself. For example, a guy's online dating profile photos include a meme of a hot couple and a quote that says, "He backed her up against the wall, boxing her in, leaning so close that their chests touched. He pressed his hands against the wall on either side of her head. Getting this close to her was dangerous and stupid and delicious all at once." You "heart" that photo to match with him and add the message, "ALL OF THIS!" You're reacting to his daring photo in a fearless way, communicating you desire a boldly affectionate man, too. That's a bold reaction and revelation, and a courageous indirect compliment.

10. The Doppelganger Approach

A doppelganger is a famous person that closely resembles someone you know or meet, in your opinion. Women have told me I look like actor Will Arnett, so he would be my doppelganger.

Say you meet a man at happy hour and it occurs to you that he reminds you of Bradley Cooper, for example. So, you ask him, "Has anyone ever told you that you look *just* like Bradley Cooper?" Whether he says yes or no, compliment the doppelganger you selected for him. "I think Bradley Cooper is the sexiest man alive."

You just indirectly communicated to him that you think *he's* incredibly sexy, and did so in a way that's creative, unique, and less threatening for both of you. He will be much more likely to engage in conversation with you, and you'd better believe he will remember how your compliment made him feel.

11. Witty Wordplay and Sexual Innuendo

Both wordplay and sexual innuendos can be fun and effective, by taking a man's words out of context and using them to flirt with him. This is a brainy way to break the ice and turn an ordinary conversation into flirtatious fun.

Example 1: You're texting with a guy at night when he says, "I gotta go. Have a doctor's appointment in the morning." You text back, "I wish I could go with you!" He texts back, "Trust me, it's not going to be fun. Annual physical." You quickly realize the word "physical" can be twisted into a sexual connotation, and text him back, "I wouldn't mind giving you a physical," followed by a winking smiley face emoticon. That's a great use of a sexual innuendo.

Example 2: You're checking out a guy's online dating profile and see a rugged photo of him wearing jeans and camouflage while fishing. You message him something like, "I bet you have a sultry Southern accent to match your manly camouflage. Do you like to fish?"

Obviously, he likes to fish, but you're fishing for bait you can use to hook him. See how I just used the words "fishing" and "bait" and "hook"—all fishing terms—but twisted them to give them a different meaning? That's witty foreplay.

He messages you back about his Southern accent, compliments you, says he loves to go bass fishing, and asks, "Do you like to fish?" You reply, "Yes, but only if they're tall, dark, and handsome." (Insert "winking" emoticon.) You're insinuating you prefer to fish for hotties like him. Clever.

Example 3: You're messaging with a lawyer and he suggests meeting you in person. You could say, "You mean like a 'trial' date, Counselor?"

Don't use that line unless you want to be judged, guilty of not being very original, and deserving of a life sentence…see what I did there? Even some corniness can be a mighty weapon in your dating tool kit.

Strive to make your chosen guy laugh. Being perceived as genuinely fun and funny is an exceedingly attractive trait. Never underestimate the power of humor. Once an emotional connection has been made, exchange numbers and continue flirting with him until he asks you out, or you ask him out.

12. The Proving Him Wrong Approach

The idea here is to look for an opportunity to prove a man wrong, just for fun. For example, if a man's online dating profile says he's not into playing games, you could message him something like, "Life is a game. Do you not like living?" You are taking his words out of context, turning a downer into an upper, and teasing him.

Again, establishing an *emotional* connection should be creative, spontaneous, flirty, and fun—not expected, logical, and boring.

Once you've proved him wrong once, and you did it in an unexpected way that was fun, you've set a precedent for the future when he decides you're mistaken about something else, or you want to try something and he doesn't. Remind him about the "game" example when you first met to imply you're right most of the time.

13. The Insincere Apology

The insincere apology, or take back, is great for when you've already given a man a bold compliment and feel like you might've come on a little *too* strong, but you're not really sorry.

Example 1: Let's say you really like a guy. But he's not great at spelling or grammar, and you've been giving him a hard time about it. He promises to improve. And you say, "It's cool. If your grammar gets too far out of line, I'll just have to spank you. With my words, of course." That last phrase, "With my words, of course," is a take back. You might mean you'll *actually* spank him with your hand, but that last part softens it a little. The insincere apology kills two birds with one stone. It's designed to seem like you are apologizing, while simultaneously doubling down on your original statement.

Example 2: You stumble across a guy's Facebook profile and start looking at his photos. You're feeling extra bold tonight, so you decide to "like" five or ten of them—a clear sign that you like what you see. Next, you send him a private message, "Sorry I liked so many of your photos. I know that goes against the "rules," but I'm a bit of a rebel." You're not really apologizing. You're using an apology as an excuse to flirt with him and tell him more about you.

Example 3: You're checking out a man's online dating profile late one night, and you're feeling sassy, so you message him something like, "Mmm ... you look yummy." (A bold compliment.) The following day, you decide to message him again, "Oh geez, that's what happens when I message a man I'm attracted to after a few glasses of wine. I apologize." (You just complimented him again.) He writes back, "Apology accepted. Truthfully, getting your message first thing this morning woke me up more than coffee ever could have!" Give him your number and you two are off to the races.

14. The Just Be Yourself Approach

Mix and match all of these approaches, a few of them, or ignore them and just be YOU.

There are countless ways to approach men in person, or to initiate a conversation online. The best way to get started is to just do it. Loosen up and speak your mind more often. Use your creativity and your imagination, and you'll differentiate yourself from other women in desirable ways, and get further faster.

If you think about approaching a man or messaging him first, but decide not to because you are afraid of how he might react, know this: the regret that comes from letting your fear of being rejected prevent you from taking any action is a hundred times worse than actually being rejected. You don't want to be the woman who's home alone and kicking herself for failing to take appropriate action, while a bolder woman is out having the time of her life with a great guy who could've been yours. The worst way to fail with men is to fail to launch.

Tip: If a man isn't interested in you, and says so politely, such as: "Thank you for the compliment, but I'm not interested," don't take it personally. Thank him for being open and honest with you, and move on.

If a man shows interest in you and you're not interested, acknowledge his effort, shoot him straight, and give him closure. For instance, "Thank you for the compliment, but you are really not my type." It may be tempting to lie or to say nothing, because you don't want to hurt his feelings. But the truth is actually the most loving and helpful thing you can say.

> "No matter how difficult and painful it might be,
> nothing sounds as good to the soul as the truth."
>
> —MARTHA BECK

Tip: If you've been put in the friend zone a time or two, here's the key to staying out of it. Stop treating men the way "just friends" treat each other. For example, friends don't usually gaze into each other's eyes and smile, or flirt with each other, or touch each other, or joke about romantic matters. If you want a man to see you as "more than a friend potential," then stop treating him like "just a friend" and up the ante.

Again, most men aren't used to being approached by women in person, or receiving a bold compliment in a woman's first message online, so the odds of him being impressed by your gesture are definitely in your favor. Even if he's not interested in you, it's great practice for the inevitable man who *will* be interested and may eventually become the love of your life.

Revisit these customizable ways to flirt with men as often as you'd like. You'll know you're on the right track when men begin telling you they are mind blown by your willingness to show them a different side of you.

When a man confesses he's extremely impressed by your creativity and confidence, smile and say thank you, or say, "It's a gift," and continue to amaze him. Or say something bold like, "You ain't seen nothing yet." For most men, backbone and daring compliments will leave them wondering, "Where have you been all my life?"

Chapter 7

ONLINE DATING MASTERY

"If there is any one secret of success, it lies in the ability to get the other person's point of view and see things from that person's angle as well from your own."

—HENRY FORD

An online dating profile is essentially an advertisement that markets your "product" (you) and your "services" to your target audience—the brand of man you want to meet.

As a fifteen-year advertising and marketing specialist for high profile corporations, I can assure you that *how* you position yourself online can significantly increase or decrease your chances of attracting, meeting, and dating the best man possible.

For example, a three-second glance at a woman's online dating profile can tell a potential mate if she's presenting someone who's a sweet, sexy, thoughtful woman with a ton of amazing qualities to offer one lucky guy or a lazy, spoiled, entitled, or ineffective communicator.

Online, you could be a ten who comes across as a seven, or a seven who comes across as a ten. Of course, who you really are still matters the most. But the persona you represent at that particular snapshot in time matters too, because if your profile doesn't immediately stand out in a desirable way, it's a swipe left.

Note: The 10-point scale is a metaphor. As you will see in Chapters 8 and 10, something is only offensive if you *choose* to *make* it offensive. Let's just face it—males and females size each other up, numerically or otherwise. It's simply a natural process.

A great online dating profile will result in more matches, likes, winks, favorites, and flirtatious messages from high quality men—giving both of you a head start on creating a magnetic mutual attraction before you even get to meet in real life. This is key because relationships are built on momentum. A strong start sets both of you up for a successful first few days or weeks of engaging and getting to know each other through your preferred dating app, or by text or phone, before scheduling your first face-to-face meeting. Once you finally connect in person, you two can pick up where you last left off and hit the ground running while everyone else is stuck playing the awkward and tedious interview game.

An attractive profile (and messaging strategy) will be one of your biggest secrets to going from first date to first kiss, to planning more rendezvous and creating a real relationship with a great guy, and perhaps, eventually falling in love.

3 Keys to Creating Irresistible Online Dating Profiles

1. Quality Photos of You

Your main profile picture is the first thing men will see, so it absolutely *must* make a great first impression. Of course, it should be one of your best photos, such as a professional headshot or full-length body shot of you smiling or at least looking friendly and approachable. It's important to select a photo your *target audience* finds very attractive, as opposed to an image of yourself that you happen to like best. Remember, your profile is a promotion for you directed at the type of man you want to meet. Therefore, it's less important what you, your mom, or a girlfriend thinks about your profile. If you're not sure which photos to use, ask for the opinion of a male friend with high standards, or you can even arrange for me to coach you. A flirtatious first photo in a cocktail dress, naturally, can be very appealing. Men are very visually oriented, so, if it is what you would normally do, showing some of your better attributes isn't a bad idea. Make sure you stay true to yourself as you decide whether you want to portray yourself most as classy, spicy, mysterious, or just plain fun!

Avoid group photos. Anything that could confuse a man, like making your first picture a group photo of you and your girlfriends, is a huge mistake. Guys see a group photo and think, *Which one is you?* I've seen online dating profiles in which all six photos are group photos. That's insane! It's *your* online dating profile, so *you* should be the star. Most men never get to your description: "I'm the one on the left." They have moved on.

If you *do* decide to use a group photo with your girlfriends, make sure *you* are the most attractive woman of the group because many men *will* compare you to your girlfriends. The last thing you should want is for the men you're trying to attract to be thinking, *Wow, I'd love to meet her girlfriend!*

Aim for six quality pictures of yourself that show different aspects of your personality. Men want to see variety, just like you do. It may be easier for you to look sultry than smiley, but endeavor to do both. Not smiling at all can make you look more masculine than what you probably want to present.

It's also crucial that you look similar in all of your photos. If a woman's weight fluctuates drastically in her pictures, most men will assume that today she's presently at the heavier weight, otherwise she wouldn't have included that photo. Make sure they are fairly current, too.

Your goal is to show men that you're a multi-faceted woman. Here are some examples you can pattern your profile after. Your first photo is a classy and sexy professional image, demonstrating you're at your best in both of these arenas. In your second photo, you're running or hiking, demonstrating you are fit, fun, and adventurous. Your third photo is a little more casual or even risqué—should you choose that route—showboating in a bikini, or doing a yoga pose in shorts and a sports bra. Your fourth is a photo of you with your dog. The fifth is you overlooking the Golden Gate Bridge in San Francisco or another travel venue. A sixth might be a group photo with your family (or your girlfriends). A variety of this nature really helps tell the story of who the real you actually is.

Make sure *you* are in all of your photos. Men do not want to see a picture of your dog, your favorite vacation spot, your car, or your home unless you're in the picture, too. Again, don't be afraid to show off your best assets. After all, dating is about love, chemistry, and attraction.

Put your best foot forward with confidence, class, and style. If your photos aren't visually appealing to him, you're not likely to get the opportunity to interact or flirt with him in a way that could lead to a first date, a serious relationship, and so much more. But don't go overboard. The idea is to look tempting, not flashy (unless you are a flashy woman). You want to tease his imagination, not give away the farm. Balance is key. Classy men like classy women who understand how to walk that fine line between looking like a lady and a sexy woman. **If a man doesn't immediately feel a strong attraction to you, he's not very likely to pursue you. On the other hand, if he doesn't respect you, he's not as likely to want a serious relationship with you.**

If you're not as foxy or as confident as you'd like to be, do *not* come out and say so. Own what you've got because self-confidence is a huge turn-on for men, too. A curvier woman who feels sexy and acts like it will generate a lot more romantic interest than a fitter woman who's insecure about her body and continually talks about this.

If you don't have enough photos of yourself that you really like, or they're mostly all group photos, start taking more individual pics, especially when looking extra fit, flirty, or just outright fabulous. Hire a professional photographer if you need to. Where there's a will there's a way, so make it happen. Your relationship future depends on it.

2. Your Profile Description

Most people mistakenly believe their online dating profile details should be all about them. However, an effective "advertisement" or "promo" must accomplish two things simultaneously:

1. It must tell your target audience—beta-dominant (or balanced) men—key aspects about yourself and what you are looking for in a man.

2. It must do so in a way that also communicates the benefits *the reader* will receive—in this case, how you can meet the needs, wants, and desires of the right man for you.

When men read your online dating profile, they're essentially pondering, "Could this relationship possibly work for me? How will I benefit from pursuing you? What makes you different in a desirable way?" Many women write self-focused profile descriptions like: "What makes me happy is playing with my dog, doing yoga, going to concerts, and sipping drinks on a patio. I like to nerd out on books, too. You have to make me laugh." That is all quite important but not sufficient to bring forth your desired results.

When men see a profile like this, they probably think, *Okay, now I know what makes her happy, and that I must make her laugh. But what is she offering me in return? Is she selfish? Does she not real-*

ize I have needs, wants, and desires, too? A description that is only focused on what you want and expect, and not how a man can also benefit from being in a relationship with you, can lead a man to assume you're self-absorbed, even though that may be the furthest thing from reality.

Instead, write your profile description in a way that combines who you are and what you are looking for, along with specific attributes a man will find very enticing. That's marketing 101.

Here's a quick example of a profile a classy Midwestern woman might write:

> *Hi! I'm a Midwestern girl with an adventurous spirit,*
> *a love for my family and friends, and I'm looking for*
> *a guy who can make me laugh. I'm a sucker for a man*
> *in jeans and cowboy boots who will take me dancing.*
> *You don't have to be any good, but you do have to hold*
> *my hand and twirl me around. I'm not into hookups,*
> *so if that's what you want, don't waste your time. I'm*
> *the real deal and I'm ready for love!*

Here's the play-by-play of why this profile description might work well for her:

- She states who she is—all positive traits most beta men probably appreciate.
- She states what kind of man she prefers—giving men info about what she's looking for and how to make her happy. (The right man for her will find this attractive.)
- She politely states what she's *not* looking for—hopefully sending those blokes running for the hills. This also lets commitment-minded men know that she's serious.
- She's leading men to take the lead by making it easier and more attractive for them to do so.

But what if you don't know what to say? Not writing anything about yourself and leaving your bio blank is also a mistake, because it doesn't give men any clues about who you are and what you offer them. If all they have to go on is your looks, that doesn't give them sufficient material to work with, should they decide to message you. The goal is to make your profile as attractive as possible, and that includes making it easier, not harder, for men to get to know you and message you with confidence.

As an alpha woman, you may prefer to be short and to the point, or use bullet points, so you can keep things moving and accomplish more. But many beta men enjoy writing and articulating their thoughts and emotions, and will likely find your profile to be more attractive if you do the same.

If you've been known to start your profile description with something like, "I hate writing about myself, but I'm an adventurous single mom . . ." Delete the preface, "I hate writing about myself, but"—and continue with more confidence this time.

"Finish This Sentence"-Style Profile Descriptions

Many dating apps today, like Bumble and Hinge, have done away with traditional profile descriptions and replaced them with a list of "finish this sentence" conversation starters, such as:

- We'll get along if…
- The best way to ask me out is…
- The three things that make a relationship great are…

It's best to choose conversation starters that are positive in nature. This will allow you to tell men who you are and what's important to you, and make it easier for you to communicate specific benefits *the right man for you will receive* if he dates you. The following examples of optional conversation starters first show an "eh" answer, and then how it could be rewritten to strengthen its appeal to your readers.

My dream dinner guest is… *Tom Hanks*
My dream dinner guest is… *my future husband!*

After work you can find me… *at the gym*
After work you can find me… *working out, walking my dog, and looking for a great guy like you!*

The best way to ask me out is… *to ask me out!*
Note: I suggest you not select this conversation starter because it is based on the alpha man-beta woman paradigm, and could be a huge turnoff for many beta-dominant men.

The key to my heart is… *tacos*
The key to my heart is… *little things like flowers or opening a door or leaving little notes*

Don't hate me if… *I'm usually 15 minutes late*
Don't hate me if… *I give you the best hug you've ever had*

My pet peeve…
Note: I also suggest you stay away from this conversation starter, because it is negatively oriented.

Together we could… *eat, drink, and chill*
Together we could… *go dancing, play board games, cook, watch movies, laugh, flirt, and teach each other new things*

The sign of a great first date… *I want to see you again*
The sign of a great first date… *we can't take our eyes off each other and don't want the night to end :)*

You should *not* go out with me if… *you don't like to travel*
You should *not* go out with me if… *you're not up for an epic adventure!*

Note: If you are a high alpha woman and you've previously had your heart set on meeting a high alpha man, you would be wise to tweak your online dating profile description(s) to be more in line with the qualities you desire in a strong beta man.

Say you're a doctor and your current profile says, "I love traveling, hiking, biking, running, and am always on-the-go. Career and family oriented. Looking for an equally active man with a kick-ass career who's independent, a gentleman with no baggage, and family-oriented."

This profile could be interpreted by a high beta man as an impossible standard for him to live up to, resulting in him not even bothering to engage with you or to ask you out, despite the fact that he *does* find you attractive and would love to meet you. Again, a man cannot be both alpha-dominant and beta-dominant, so it's best to communicate what you are looking for in a mostly beta (or balanced) man.

For example, you might tweak your profile to say, "I'm a foodie who loves to travel, but that does NOT mean I expect you to pay for my flights, drinks, and meals, LOL. I'm looking for a life partner, not a sugar daddy. I'm full of energy and stay pretty busy. But after a long day, I want to relax and cuddle with my man while watching Netflix. I'm not looking for a rich guy, either. As long as you work hard at your job, you're family oriented, and promise to treat me right, I guarantee you'll be treated well, too. Sound good? Then stop reading my profile and say hello!"

Every word you write should be unique, fun, funny, interesting, optimistic, flirtatious, smart, sexy, loving, and/or partnership-focused! If any aspect of your profile could be perceived *by men* as selfish, lazy, boring, negative, or based on the alpha man-beta woman paradigm, you need to delete it and rewrite it.

Remember, you're not trying to impress *everyone*. You're only trying to impress the types of beta-dominant (or balanced) men you want to meet. Write your profile like it's a letter to one man, as opposed to hundreds or thousands of men. This way every man who reads your profile will feel like you're talking to him and him alone.

Implementing these strategic communication tips will make your online dating profile(s) considerably more attractive to quality men, resulting in more matches, enthusiastic messages, and exciting first dates for you.

3. Have Multiple Online Dating Profiles

There are way too many dating apps to even attempt to cover them all. But I strongly recommend using at least two or three simultaneously. Whatever profile options each offers, do your best to use them instead of leaving them blank. Most dating apps also have additional features available for purchase, usually relating to making your profile more visible, accelerating your path to letting a man know you're interested in him, or providing additional privacy like being able to search and see who's already "liked" you without men knowing that you checked them out.

I recommend newer dating apps like Hinge, Bumble, The League, Coffee Meets Bagel, and Inner Circle, but if you are concerned that these are "elitist" apps, or there isn't a lot of participation in your city, more well-known dating apps could be your best bet. Feel free to experiment based on your demographics and psychographics, such as your age, personal values, and beliefs.

If you're a Christian woman in your 50s, you might sign up for Christian Mingle, eHarmony, and Our Time. If you're in your late 30s or 40s, you might pay for a Match membership, or Elite Singles, but also use Tinder. If you're African American, you might include Black People Meet. If you're Jewish, JDate is popular.

Using multiple sites or apps gives you the opportunity to use different photo combinations and profile descriptions. Even professional advertisers and marketers need to test different messages and photos to see what works best. The same may be true for you. If one approach isn't working, try a different one *until* you get the results you're looking for.

Fishing for men in several different dating ponds also increases your chances of catching Mr. Right. More "fishing poles" plus more enticing "bait" equals a better chance of reeling one in for the record books!

Tip: Facebook and Instagram aren't technically dating apps, but many singles use them like one. As a single man, private messaging women is frowned upon by some women. But as a woman, sending a direct message to a man you're attracted to is much more acceptable. In fact, I recommend it. If a guy adds you as a "friend" on Facebook (or you add him), and you're intrigued by him, private message him—quickly. Compliment him. Be funny or flirtatious. Use emoticons. If the conversation goes well and there's clearly chemistry, go "like" or "love" a few of his photos *while* you're messaging back and forth. Keep it up and you're probably going on an exciting date soon. Who knows? He could be "the one."

How to Message Men First Like a Boss

Once your profile is set up, it's time to start searching for and interacting with men. Here's where understanding the Law of Polarity—you go first—and the Law of Reciprocation will give you an advantage over other women, and accelerate your online dating success with men. When it comes to searching for and messaging men, most women have a "sit back and wait for the guys to approach" attitude and dating philosophy. On dating apps like Bumble, where women *must* go first, many women lead with terrible first messages like:

> "Hi."
>
> "What's up?"
>
> "Good morning."
>
> "Hey John, how's your week going?"

These openers are *instant* attraction-killers. Chemistry is emotional, not rational. And there's *zero* emotional appeal in any of these. The goal is to be different in a desirable way, and these are the exact opposite—generic, boring, and lazy.

Saying, "Good morning" or "Hey, how's your week going?" is fine when texting with a male you've already established a strong emotional connection with. But when you first message a man, you don't know each other at all. Therefore, you must lead with clear strength, not weakness. Plus, due to the Law of Reciprocation, if you say, "Hey," he's probably going to say, "Hey." If you say, "Hi, how's your week going?" He's probably going to say, "Great, how's your week going?" In addition to being boring, the ball is now back in *your* court. Instead of taking the lead and messaging him back in a unique way, many alpha women sit back and then wonder why he's not stepping up. He's not stepping up because he already responded and now it's your turn again. It's also more difficult for him to react in a substantial way if you don't give him something solid to react to.

In the dating world of alpha men and beta women, it might be okay to say, "Hi," and then expect the man to take the lead. But in the dating world of alpha women and beta men, you are the leader and he will be the responder.

Tip: Treat *every* dating app or site as if it were Bumble, where *you* must go first. For example, on Hinge, even if you accepted his match request and invited him to start the chat, you will get far better results faster by starting the chat yourself.

In an exchange of ten shared messages with a man going back and forth, ideally, you will message him first, third, fifth, seventh, and ninth—possibly ending with *you* suggesting a first meeting. And he will message you second, fourth, sixth, eighth, and tenth—*him* saying, "Great, I can't wait to meet you!" In short, you go, then he goes. Changing your online communications to align with the alpha woman–beta man paradigm, where you're the leader and beta men are the responders, will transform your dating life, fast.

From now on, I suggest you proactively search for the men you're interested in online, and initiate a conversation using one of several possible approaches, like combining the awareness approach with the flattery approach—by checking out a man's photos and reading his profile description, and then paying him a bold compliment in a way that's going to come across as unique to him. This demonstrates you took the time to actually study his profile and learn a little about him, and that you're interested in him specifically, not just any man who might respond.

In person, we all love people with positive emotions. Since he can't see your facial expressions online, you will want to make sure your *written* text expresses your current feelings and state of mind.

For example, no period at the end of a sentence demonstrates laziness, whereas a period shows attention to detail. Exclamation points show excitement! Ellipses portray mystery … or curiosity. A smiley face reinforces a happy thought. A wink can be used in a variety of ways, like being sarcastic or flirty. The fire symbol can be used to say, "You're hawt!" Expressions of this nature can be very powerful.

Whatever you want to communicate, do it in a creative, expressive way, and there are countless bonus points to be earned. Remember, the name of the game is to differentiate yourself in desirable and creative ways.

The following example shows how you'd instantly feel way more attraction for one man over another, simply because of his first message to you.

Example: Let's say you are wearing a ravishing red dress in one of your online dating profiles. The first guy messages you, *Hey, how's your week going?"* The second guy messages you, *"Hi Jennifer! There's nothing sexier to me than a beautiful woman in a stunning red dress. I* *see you like to work out, too. Do you ever go running at XYZ local park? Duke, my golden retriever, loves it when we go there!*

Which of these two approaches makes you feel the best and makes a lasting first impression? Obviously, the second message is a hundred times better than the first—not just because it makes you feel pretty amazing, but because you now have specific details and insights to work with in your response. You know he thinks you're stunning, so you're likely to compliment him on his looks, too. You also know a favorite running spot of his, and that he has a golden retriever named Duke. From that one message alone, you know enough to start thinking about a first date at the local park—versus the first guy's message, which tells you absolutely nothing, adds no value whatsoever, and one to which you probably won't even reply. This is why nailing the first message is crucial to go from "swipe right" to flirting, to exchanging numbers, to planning your first date, to sharing your first kiss, and so on.

Let's look at three examples of excellent first messages to see how *you* might message a man first to get the ball rolling.

Example 1: You see a picture of him standing next to the Eiffel Tower in Paris, and you've been there, too. You use the awareness approach to establish a common interest and pay him a bold compliment. You message him, *Hi John! I see you've been to the City of Light. Paris is SO romantic! You're VERY handsome. I bet the French women couldn't take their eyes off of you.*

Example 2: It's a few weeks before Christmas, so you start with, *Hey Josh, I can't wait for Christmas! Have you been a good boy this year?* You're being flirtatious in a topical way. Great start!

Example 3: Scott's Bumble profile says, *I love going to ball games and concerts. I am awesome at grilling steaks and parallel parking. I'm a sucker for a good-looking woman in a ball cap, jeans, and a tank top. You gotta love dogs. Ralph and I are a package deal. Let's meet up and grab a beer!*

Note: This last profile is somewhat self-focused, but it also lists many benefits for female readers. Most women like going to ball games and concerts; appreciate a man who can grill her a steak dinner; and who's a skillful driver. A man with a dog can be very attractive, too, because this demonstrates extra responsibility in his life, and because he probably has a fun side with the pet thing going on.

You make a few mental notes: Ball games, grilling steaks, and dog. You message him:

> *Hey Scott! Do you mind if I call you Scottie the Hottie? That's what first came to my mind when I read your profile and saw your cute smile.*
>
> *You should've seen the look on my puppy, Ginger's, face when I showed her your pictures. She started wagging her tail like crazy! We should have a barbeque soon and see who makes the best steaks. Ginger would love to meet you and Ralph, too!*
>
> *But first, what did you like best about my profile? If your answer is as good as your photos, let's grab a beer soon and see if we click. If you're lucky, I might even wear my favorite ball cap and tank top for you.—Jenny*

Note: This message might be longer than what you're used to writing, but that could also make it stand out in a desirable way. The only "rule" here is to throw away the old rules and be your authentic self—a go-getter who's interesting, passionate, and enthusiastic. You're an alpha who can act like one anywhere and anytime you choose. Also, remember to hit the return key to space out your sentences, which will increase readability.

Here's the play-by-play of why this first message might work well for her:

Hey Scott! Do you mind if I call you Scottie the Hottie? That's what first came to my mind when I read your profile and saw your cute smile.

You complimented him in a way that's unique to him; spoke your mind in a way that can't be faked; showed him you can communicate in a flirty way; and you've already given him an endearing nickname.

You should've seen the look on my puppy's face when I showed her your pictures. Her tail started wagging like crazy!

You demonstrated you actually read his profile, found and established common ground—the fact that you both have a dog—and you used a clever language trick, speaking in the third person, to compliment him once more.

Tip: Using third person is an excellent way to communicate bold things you might not normally say in the first person. A bold compliment from your dog, for example, could be even more powerful than a direct compliment from you. He knows it's coming from you, but it's creative, original, and can be less awkward than a direct compliment when first getting to know a guy. Plus, should he not like your flattery, you can save face by blaming Ginger.

We should have a barbeque soon and see who makes the best steaks.

You're subtly suggesting a possible first date. It sounds like a bet—who can grill the best steaks? What man wouldn't be impressed by a woman who's confident enough to imply she can give him a run for his money with BBQ skills? Even if you've never grilled a steak in your life, it's your confidence that counts. Even if you burn your steak, you two can laugh about it while sharing a bottle of merlot.

Ginger would love to meet you and Ralph, too! But first, what did you like best about my profile?

Now he knows your dog's name, you paid him another compliment, and asked him a question designed to get him to open up and reveal what he liked about your profile. Well done!

Tip: Once you've communicated genuine interest in a man, invite him to reciprocate, if he doesn't do so on his own. If he doesn't, consider moving on. If he does, listen carefully and make mental notes for future reference.

If your answer is as good as your photos, let's grab a beer soon and see if we click. If you're lucky, I might even wear my favorite ball cap and tank top for you.

See how you're challenging him to come up with a great answer? You're also offering a reward if he passes your test—drinks and quality time with you, the *real* prize—plus, the opportunity to see you in a ball cap and a tank top, which he stated is a huge turn on for him, demonstrating you listen well and quickly take cues.

Consider signing your name. Even if it is listed on your dating profile, you should want him to see your name again and again. You want him to start thinking about nicknames he might call you, or you can give yourself one that mirrors the nickname you gave him.

Use his name too—it's the most important word for each of us.

When it comes to the importance of initiating a conversation with a man from a position of strength, there's no specific technique you must follow. You're simply taking the time to genuinely get to know a little bit about him, and demonstrating you took the time to do so, complimenting him, expressing your interest, and finding and establishing common ground. You've put your best foot forward, freeing him to reciprocate in a similar fashion. Before you know it, you'll both be ready to exchange numbers and start planning your first get together.

Tip: A man messages you first and his profile piques your interest, but he leads with something boring and expected like, "Hey Susan, what's up?" Your best bet is to ignore his first message and send him a new message based on the strategies we just covered. For example, "Hey Mike, I love your green pants! You're sexy and you know it."

Challenge: Revise your online dating profiles and start messaging men first. Compliment them. See if they reciprocate in a similar way. Then it's your turn again. Don't sit back and wait for guys to always take the lead. It's much better, with your skill set, that you stay in the lead, or lead him to lead you by messaging him something like, "Have you tried XYZ Mexican restaurant on Main Street? I hear they have the best queso dip and frozen margaritas." When it's time to arrange your first in person meeting, he will likely suggest that Mexican restaurant. Now you have a hot date and you also get to go where *you* wanted to go!

Chapter 8

EXCHANGING NUMBERS, FIRST DATES, AND BEYOND

"The most dangerous phrase in the language is
'we've always done it this way.'"

—GRACE HOPPER

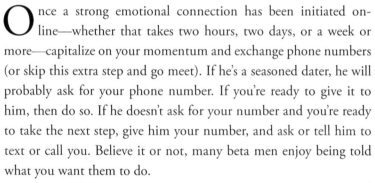

O nce a strong emotional connection has been initiated on-line—whether that takes two hours, two days, or a week or more—capitalize on your momentum and exchange phone numbers (or skip this extra step and go meet). If he's a seasoned dater, he will probably ask for your phone number. If you're ready to give it to him, then do so. If he doesn't ask for your number and you're ready to take the next step, give him your number, and ask or tell him to text or call you. Believe it or not, many beta men enjoy being told what you want them to do.

You could also anticipate how you want a man to respond, and bait him into asking for your number online by messaging something like, "You should call me sometime." According to the Law of Reciprocation, he might say, "I'd love to, but I don't have your number." Then you give it to him. That's leading him to do what you want him to.

Texting or Talking on the Phone

Ideally, he will call or text you in the next 24 hours. It might be right away, or he might wait a little while. Be patient and give him time to make his move. If he doesn't call or text you within 24 hours, it doesn't mean he doesn't like you. Maybe he's not sure what to say next. If you have his number too, take the lead and text or call him, and start strong again. Compliment him or express that you'd really like to meet him. You're the leader, remember? If you've ever said or thought, "I don't want to lead," realize that's the same thing as saying, "I don't want to be myself." Be the change you wish to see in your dating life.

You don't have to wait for him to ask for a date, either. You could take charge and suggest a day, time, and place to meet.

How to Use Social Media to Do First-Date Recon

If you want to do some due diligence on a man before you meet him, either to make sure he is who he says he is, or to learn more about him in preparation for your first date, the Internet is your helpful friend.

Without a phone number or even his name, you can save an image from his online dating profile, crop it, upload it to Google Image, and see if someone has used that particular profile picture on their social media. If that same picture is being used on any other website, it will pop up in the results and you'll be able to learn a little more about him through his social media profiles.

Note: This is also super useful when you suspect someone is catfishing you and is using fake profile pictures. You will be able to tell if it's really *his* picture, or if the person stole a photo or series of photos from a modeling website or other online personality. Generally, when they're all "model" pictures, you can guarantee it's someone with a fake profile.

With a first name and phone number, but no last name, you can do an online search for his number or enter it on Facebook, and then look for his name and photo to learn his last name. You can then browse his Facebook photos, or look for him on LinkedIn and see his work history. If you don't want him to see that you viewed his LinkedIn profile, ask a friend to look for you. Maybe you will be able to find a complementary business skill, or one or two things you have in common, and "randomly" mention it during your first meeting. You might also, through some other online search, learn he's divorced and has three kids, something he "conveniently" left off his Bumble profile, and you decide to stop messaging him.

Once you save a man's number in your cell phone, his Facebook profile may also pop up when you do a search for "people you might know" or "suggested friends." If all you have is his first name, type it into the search bar of Facebook and add "in Seattle" or whichever city or town you're in. If he has a unique name, even better. Then look for pictures of him.

Three Possible Texting, Talking, and Flirting "Pitfalls" to Be Aware of

1. Being Extra Sensitive Early in the Morning

Have you ever noticed you're often more whimsical at night, and more critical of yourself or others in the morning? For example, maybe you might tend to check your online dating profiles and flirt more during the evening, and are more business-minded first thing in the morning. You might have hooked up with a hot guy one night, after a *few* drinks. Looking back, it seemed like a really good idea at the time, but the next morning you felt awful about it and judged yourself rather harshly. Then as the day went on, you felt better and better about it, and decided it wasn't such a bad idea after all. In fact, it was pretty fun and you might even want to do it again!

In case you are wondering *why* this happens, it's likely largely due to circadian rhythms—defined as, "physical, mental, and behavioral changes that follow a daily cycle"[50]—which are linked to our psychological characteristics. Our minds, emotions, and overall physiology fluctuate, even hour to hour. At peak circadian arousal times, your brain power is at its highest. If you are a morning person (many alpha women are), your brain power may be at its highest then, and vice versa for a person who's more of a night owl (many beta men are).

Many alpha women are logical thinkers (often left-brain dominant), and many beta men are more emotionally driven (often right-brain dominant). If you are a morning person, *you* may be even *more* logical and reality-based first thing in the morning, and *they* may be even *more* emotional, creative, and expressive late at night—again, you are polar opposites.

Taking this as a basis, as an alpha woman, flirting with creative beta men will typically be the most fun for you because they tend to be more witty, playful, and impulsive. However, messaging with them late at night can also lead to a perfect storm the next morning.

Let's say you're both up late texting each other and flirting. He's being witty and pushing the envelope a little with sexual innuendo. You're enjoying each other immensely, but it's time to say goodnight because you have to be up at 6 a.m. So, *you* text goodnight and turn off your phone. But *he* stays up later and decides to text you something even more saucy.

The next morning, when you are in an extremely logical mode, the same type of message you thought was funny or enticing the night before might now seem highly inappropriate. You could easily feel offended and think, *How dare he say something like that to me. We just met!*

He may or may not have said anything "wrong." You are simply interpreting his messages differently because your *brain state* changed. If you're not aware that you may be far more sensitive and reproving first thing in the morning, you could easily choose to end all communication with a great beta guy who could've been your soulmate.

If you suspect you might get triggered far more easily in the morning, you may not want to check your text messages from men you're talking to and flirting with until later in the day, or at least be aware that you could tend to be somewhat defensive first thing in the morning. Understanding yourself and respecting these key differences will give you a much better chance of meeting and keeping the right man and working together for your mutual benefit.

2. Literal versus Metaphorical Interpretations

Different people often interpret the exact same words differently. Extremely and mostly beta men often use analogies and metaphors to express an *intended* thought or idea, whereas extremely and mostly alpha women are usually more direct and often take things literally.

For example, when I first marketed my coaching program, my written sales pitch told alpha women they would learn a "dirty little secret" about men and dating. Many women asked me, "What's *dirty* about it?" Nothing. The phrase "dirty little secret" is a figure of speech that means the same thing as a "little-known secret."

I also told women my program would give them an "unfair advantage" over other single women in their area. Many asked me, "What's *unfair* about it?" Nothing. An "unfair advantage" is another figure of speech that means an advantage that's so big, it's almost unfair.

These misinterpretations might seem like really small things. But when you're first getting to know a guy on a dating app, or texting, or even on a date, and you're both hypersensitive to potential red flags and word choices, little things like this can lead *both* of you to assume the other is completely missing the point and connecting poorly.

If a charming man uses wit, sarcasm, metaphors, or analogies when engaging with you, and you don't understand what he means, use it as a learning opportunity and ask him to explain.

3. Shutting Down If a Beta Man Texts You Too Much, Too Fast

Many extremely or mostly beta-dominant men are known for overcommunicating. It's a manifestation of having an extremely or primarily "female brain," which can overwhelm their minds with random thoughts coming from every direction, particularly when they get excited. And, surely, texting with an alpha woman that they're quite attracted to qualifies as "an exciting time." Many beta men also love to talk and be heard. Thus, they might not even realize they are oversharing—they are simply "being themselves"—the same way you might not realize you could be under sharing—you are simply "being yourself."

Again, neither of you is "right" or "wrong." You're just different.

If a beta man opens up to you fast and furiously, it usually means he likes you, feels comfortable with you, and is excited to get to know you. It's simply his way of expressing these feelings. It's best taken as a compliment.

But from your perspective, an onslaught of texts or online messages may be very stressful, because it may take you longer to process your own emotions, much less his. It's simply a manifestation of having an extremely or mostly "male brain" processor. Your natural reaction may be to shut down and ignore his texts for a while, or to ghost him altogether.

The solution is pretty straightforward: You both need to be more aware of your differences, so you can work together for your mutual benefit.

Beta men need to be more aware of a possible tendency for emotional outbursts, especially when "talking to" alpha women, and make a conscious effort be a little less communicative and a little more guarded (e.g., more alpha).

Likewise, alpha women need to be more aware of a possible tendency for emotional shutdowns, especially when "talking to" beta men, and make a conscious effort to be a bit less guarded and a little more communicative (e.g., more beta).

Balance is the key.

Making Plans to Meet Each Other

Once you've texted back and forth for a day or two, or spoken on the phone, ideally, he will ask for your availability and begin thinking about a date, a time, and a good place to meet you. Tell him when you are available—a good day and general timeframe that works for you. This is leading him to plan a date.

Next, he will probably name two or three places you could meet because the "female brain" loves coming up with ideas, but isn't always so great at being decisive. Your brain, the "male brain," loves making plans, organizing logistics, and being decisive because of its structural, linear thinking process.

When a man says, "Here are three possible date locations, which would you prefer?" he's being thoughtful and trying to please you. He is not being lazy or indecisive. He took the initiative to suggest several options and present them to you. It's best not to respond with something like, "I don't know, what do you want to do?" Or "I'd prefer you decide and tell me when and where."

Be yourself and make his life a hundred times easier by picking one of the places he suggested—whichever you prefer—and then say something like, "Great, let's meet this Sunday at 6 p.m. Does that work for you?"

Another option is for you to take the lead well before he goes to the trouble of researching possible places to meet by thinking of a place you love and saying something like, "I know a great little cafe on Tenth Street. Would you like to meet me there next Wednesday night at 7?" The more proactive you are, the more attracted he will be to you. This is also effective because you're being straightforward and communicating your desires, as opposed to making him guess what you want and hoping he guesses right, then potentially being disappointed if he guesses wrong.

How to Save What Could Have Been

If a man asks you out, but you're going out of town for a week, and he doesn't ask you out again when you get back, don't wait for him to make the next move. He already asked you out once. It's now *your turn* to reciprocate. Text or call him when you get back and express your continued desire to meet him.

If a guy asks you out and you can't make it due to a schedule conflict, or you two agree on a day and time, but later you have to cancel, the ball is now in *your* court. If you still want to meet him, don't wait for him to contact you again. Reciprocate by asking him out and plan the date yourself. No more sitting back and waiting for the man to plan all of the dates.

If men tend to ask you out at the last minute, you probably hate it because you're a busy woman who likes to plan ahead and needs more notice. You might also believe they're treating you like a last-minute option instead of a priority. I'm not giving them a total pass because they should learn to be more respectful of your time, but many beta men *aren't* good planners. To borrow from the movie *Along Came Polly*, starring Jennifer Aniston and Ben Stiller, they're on the "non-plan plan." It's a symptom of having an extremely or mostly "female brain." According to Dr. Brizendine, the "female brain" often manifests in a person being more focused on living life minute-by-minute and trying to deal with their emotional ups and downs.[51] As a result, many beta men are less structured and more impulsive. You might also find you actually like being more spontaneous now and then. If you decline every time a guy asks you out at the last minute, you may be missing out on an opportunity to meet, date, and fall in love with an amazing beta man who may be *sincerely* interested in getting to know you. It's something worth considering if you really like him. Communication is important and if you explain why you feel like you aren't a priority, and he can understand and explain his thought process, then you can both compromise a bit and still win.

Tip: If you still think about an ex, and as far as you know he's not married, why not look him up and give love a second chance? If you loved each other way back when, there's a good chance he still has feelings for you, too. (This could also apply for a high school or college crush.)

First Date Considerations

A first date (or an initial meeting) is not the time to decide if he's "the one." Just chill out a bit.

When you meet for the first time, you both may be a little nervous. That's actually a *good* sign because it means there's something riding on this date. Relax and have a good time. Ask each other fun questions like, "What are you passionate about? Where would you love to travel to and why?"

It's fine to ask him more about his life, his work, if he has any kids, or whatever you'd like to learn about him. Do not, however, make him feel like he's participating in "20 questions."

Take turns sharing about your lives, your passions, or talking about your mutual interests. Play the doppelganger game. Pay him a bold compliment or two. Engage in some witty wordplay and twist his words into a little "playfulness" if you feel like it. Laugh, flirt, and have fun.

As you get to know a man better and he begins to open up, it usually means he likes you and is excited about the possibility of dating you. If he's forthcoming about a few of his challenges in his life, it's easy to understand how you might interpret him as "weak" and be turned off, *if* you see the world through the lens of "strength versus weakness," and strive to portray strength and avoid showing weakness at all costs.

But remember, many beta men see the world through the lens of "right versus wrong," and he could easily consider honesty, humility, and transparency to be "right" or high priorities for him. Some form of hiding his weaknesses might be considered "wrong." So, keep that in mind the next time a potential guy opens up his heart and shares a few personal struggles or vulnerabilities with you, and don't just immediately write him off. His deep sharing may *actually* be a sign that he likes you and trusts you.

If you're both having a really good time, it's perfectly fine to let him know you're into him by reaching for his hand, or rubbing his arm, running your fingers across his back, or putting your hand on his knee or thigh. This all really depends on where your first date takes place, how comfortable you two are with each other, your personal values and relationship goals, and what feels right in the moment.

Yes, you could sit back and play with your hair, apply more lip-gloss and pucker your lips, or give him your best "come hither" look—signs you want him to make a move and kiss you. These are all examples of tempting a man to take the lead. But many beta men would love it if you were even more direct. As an alpha woman, you can also take the lead and make a move on him first. Or simply say, "Shut up and kiss me."

Breaking the Money Barrier:
Who Should Pay for a First Date?

"Who asks who out on the date? Who's supposed to pay
for dinner? Who chooses where you go? Both partners
should be involved in these discussions. If we want to be
treated as equals, don't put yourself in a position where you
set yourself up to not be equal."

—WHITNEY WOLFE HERD

If the early days of hunter-gatherer societies were like traditional
dating today, the beta man would go hunting and kill the food.
Then he'd carry it back to the village, start the fire, cook the meat,
serve it to you, and then do the dishes, too. Then he'd repeat this
one-sided routine every time you two get together. No matter how
nice that might sound to you, it wouldn't be a very efficient use of his
time and resources. **In reality, men and women back then *worked
together* to survive. And today, there's no reason why men and
women can't work together to make dating thrive.**

I know polite society says it's the man's "job" to pay for the first
date, and possibly every date after that. But this mental agreement
is selfish, sexist, and *the* cornerstone of the old way of doing things,
which is, to a large degree, responsible for your past and present
negative results. It's also a staple of the alpha man-beta woman
paradigm, and this entire book is about killing—or at least soften-
ing—that incongruent paradigm, and creating a new one that's in
alignment with the Law of Polarity, the Law of Reciprocation, the
Law of Differentiation, and other key principles. I suggest you throw
away this "gender rule," and replace it with a mindset, attitude, and
personal dating philosophy focused on providing value and *leading*
with love and respect.

If you went to lunch with a potential new girl or guy friend, you'd be totally put off if they expected you to pay the whole bill, wouldn't you? Dating should be no different because you're looking for a potential best friend and, possibly, the love of your life. Therefore, you should be treating your dates equally as well as a potential friend, or even more lovingly.

I totally understand why many women would love to hang onto this "rule." Financially, it's a huge advantage. *But sexism is not sexy. Equality is.* Can you imagine what it would feel like to be a single guy who goes on twenty first meetings a year, and ends up paying 100 percent for all of them, with no reassurance of mutual interest? Multiply this by several years and many guys end up paying thousands of dollars on women they're not even in a relationship with. So, women get to date for free? That doesn't sound like equality to me. Thankfully, a slight shift in perspective can pay huge dividends.

> "A good compromise is one
> where everybody makes a contribution."
>
> —ANGELA MERKEL

If you two "met" online, exchanged numbers, agreed on a time and place, and you're meeting in-person for the first time, it's not really a date—it's a first meeting—because you've never met and have no idea if you like each other. You're both there to figure that out.

Whether he asked you or you asked him, the fairest thing for everyone in this situation is to just split the bill, the same way you would if meeting a girlfriend for drinks or dinner. If he declines your offer and pays for it all, great. If he seems pleasantly surprised that you'd offer and agrees, also great. If you're feeling generous and want to treat him, more power to you.

Of course, if you *have* met in-person and he then asks you out, he should pay. If you ask him out, you should pay. If it's not clear who's asked whom, split it.

Remember that a date is an audition for a loving relationship. Ask yourself, "What is the loving thing to do?" Then do that.

The Key to Getting Off the First Date Merry-Go-Round and On with the Show

If your first meeting goes well and you *both* like each other, most men will be eager to plan and pay for a more traditional first *official* date—such as him picking you up at your place and taking you to a show, or maybe wining and dining you. But do not *expect* this. Adopt the motto: "Expect nothing, appreciate everything." Besides, maybe *you* will want to plan and pay for your first official date together.

If you two have a blast together on your first *bona fide* date and you're both eager to see each other again, if he planned and paid for the first date, you should seriously consider planning and paying for your second date together. He can then plan and pay for your third date, or whatever you two talk about and agree upon. **That's reciprocation, equality, and balance.**

In summary, treat each other like teammates. Take turns, share, and seek to win together. Treat the men you meet like they are your boyfriend or future husband, because they ultimately could be.

Tip: If you two go on a "first meeting" and you really like him, but he doesn't ask you out on an official first date, and you want another chance to impress him, ask him out and plan and pay for it. Talk about differentiation! He might be blown away by your confidence and persistence and reciprocate. If he doesn't, he probably simply doesn't "get" you, for whatever reason. But at least you will have given it your best shot. Focus on what you want and control what *you* can control.

An Honest Answer to a Question You May Have about Sex

A lot of women ask me, *Why do so many guys expect me to sleep with them so quickly?*

First and foremost, different men (and women) want different things, at different times, for different reasons. But high polarity can be a definite a factor. The stronger the magnetic "pull" toward each other, the stronger the temptation will likely be. Combine this with the facts that a large percentage of mostly alpha women are strikingly beautiful, and confident go-getters; and a lot of mostly beta men are good-looking, charming, spontaneous, and affectionate; and quality time together can "heat up" in a hurry. Many mostly beta men also *love* to pleasure a woman, and crave a lucky lady to love and to please.

Second, if a man does *not* escalate quickly enough, many women will think he doesn't like her, or that he's not "man enough" for her. Beta men are constantly being told, "Be more alpha!" Some women wish they would show a more accelerated interest, and others wish they would take it more slowly. It can all be very challenging. Maybe we should go back to "mood rings" so the signaling is abundantly clear!

Third, some beta men may be insecure about their career stability, their bank account, or their overall ability to measure up to the sky-high expectations that many mostly alpha women have for them. They may also feel social pressure to live up to the tenets of the alpha man–beta woman worldview, which is largely unrealistic and unfair to most beta men today. So, they might think, *Why should I even bother pursuing a real relationship?*

Fourth, the dating apps and hookup culture are major factors. Believe it or not, the hookup culture is very likely a *manifestation* of the traditional, outmoded dating playbook, which is essentially *backwards* for alpha females and beta males (roles reversed). A lot of guys likely got tired of having to ask alpha women out, plan their dates, and pay for them with *no* assurance of some form of reciprocation. So, they decided to skip formal dating and went right to the shortcut.

Note: Men aren't the only ones seeking "shortcuts." It also takes two to tango.

Finally, the adversarial and unbalanced courtship "rules" that *created* the hookup culture are still very much in play today. Men are likely *reacting* to how women are treating them, and vice versa.

Note: I am not excusing or blaming anyone, merely analyzing many possibilities.

Dating and relationships are supposed to be mutually beneficial and a reset is clearly in order.

The good news is that by developing romantic relationships according to this *New Dating Playbook*, and *leading* with love and respect on your outings, most men will *follow* your lead and treat you more lovingly and respectfully—which is in *both* parties' best interest.

Tip: Some of the *best* men aren't playing this game at all, and may never have. They might not even be on the dating apps. Many probably spend their nights and weekends working out, watching TV, reading books, attending religious services, and *wishing* a quality woman like you would show interest in them first, and take the lead. So, if you're tired of meeting "players" and emotionally unavailable men, then proactively look for the good-hearted, honorable men you see or meet in person, or that you're Facebook friends with, and initiate a conversation with them! Great guys who will be loyal and loving to you exist, I promise.

A Whole New Dating World

Now that you're focused on being more of a leader or co-leader, and a great potential partner, your dating success is largely in *your* hands.

Anytime you want a fun date, all you've got to do is call or text a guy and say, "I have two tickets to the Imagine Dragons concert. Would you like to join me?" Or "I've been dying to try out this new restaurant. Would you like to meet me there this Saturday night at 8 p.m.?"

On your dates, take the lead a little more and ask intriguing questions. Make mental notes for future reference. Remember what you learned about him previously. Find ways to show him you were listening, and how you feel about him. Be sure to say how much fun you're having on your dates, and lead him to ask you out for a second date by suggesting another activity you two could do together. Be far more proactive and you could be on a second or a third date, and maybe even in a promising relationship, before you know it.

If you love to travel the world, but typically go alone or with your fellow alpha girlfriends—whether it's a personal preference or because the men you meet can't afford to take you on exotic vacations—why not invite a guy you really like and split the costs? Or rent a cabin in the woods and enjoy the scenery and each other.

Once you start dating a guy, remember, most beta men want to please you and will make more of an effort, once they know what your preferences are. So, don't be afraid to tell him what you want. Let's say you two agree to meet for ice cream and the first meeting goes really well. A few days later, he calls to ask you out again and suggests meeting you at a local steakhouse for dinner. If you'd rather he pick you up at your place and drive together to the restaurant, you can just say, "Why don't you pick me up?" That's being a leader and communicating what you want. Again, beta men aim to please, so make it easier for them to please you. Help them help you.

Since his goal is to bring happiness and satisfaction your way, do *not* tell a man you *don't* want him to do something if you *do* want him to, or that you *don't* care one way or the other if you *do* care.

This is an extreme example, but let's pretend you two live in a hurricane-prone zone like South Florida; Charleston, SC; or Houston, TX. The weatherman says a Category 5 hurricane is headed your way, and you are boarding up the windows of your home.

Your new boyfriend calls and asks what you're doing, so you tell him. He asks if you want him to come over and help you, and you say, "No thanks, I got it." (Or "I don't care.")

You're probably thinking, *Why is he even asking? Of course, I want him to come over and help me, but I shouldn't have to ask him to.* A wise man would ignore your "no thanks" and come over anyway, but not all men are that astute.

If you *did* want him to come over and he didn't, you can't really blame him because you told him you *didn't* want him to. He's honoring your request. You led him to do what you *didn't* want him to do.

Again, beta men aim to please. So, if you *do* want him to do something, don't tell him you *don't* want him to. Just be honest and say, "Yes, I'd *love* your help. Bring wine, too."

Physical Escalation

When it comes to being affectionate, everyone has their own personal values and a desired timeline. But everyone wants to touch and be touched eventually, so take the following tips with a grain of salt and apply them whenever or however you'd like.

As an alpha woman, it would be exceedingly rare for you to be anything but "alpha" sexually. Don't hide your best "assets," or your inner-thoughts and outward desires simply because you've been taught you're supposed to be a "good" girl, or you're worried he won't respect you if you give him a sneak-peek of your intimate side.

Beta men's top three love languages are often quality time, physical touch, and words of affirmation. Touching him and encouraging him to touch you, while affirming him and telling him how he makes you feel, will drive him wild. As you two escalate further, you will likely learn beta men love foreplay, even more than you might. Taking your time getting to know each other is a huge turn-on for many men. But a man may also want his woman to throw caution to the wind every now and then and show him her saucy side.

As a result, you're not likely to dress or act too sensual for a strong beta man, especially in private. If you are a little more conservative, you may prefer dressing more traditionally in public. But once you're at home and it's just the two of you, feel free to lose your inhibitions.

That being said, if your goal is to be celibate until marriage, or you simply want to take your time getting to know each other and not jump into anything too quickly, tone down the arousing language, and keep your hands to yourself. This way you can focus on truly getting to know each other and making sure you actually like each other.

Regardless of your physical escalation preferences, good conversation, laughter, earning each other's trust and respect, and developing solid companionship are far better indicators of long-term connection potential than short-term fun.

Your end goal could be a healthy and happy "forever-after relationship," and there are a lot of ways to get there!

Chapter 9

CREATIVE SEDUCTION

"You are mine."

—CHRISTIAN GREY, *FIFTY SHADES* TRILOGY

Have you ever been blown away by a man's creative effort to win your heart? One minute you're thinking, *I kind of like this guy.* The next thing you know, after he does something very imaginative, you're thinking, *He makes me feel like the luckiest woman in the world!*

Your ideal man should be utilizing the following "formula" to woo you. But why wait for him to win you over? Why not make *him* feel like the luckiest man in the world because he's with you?

In this chapter, you will discover how to tap into and use your *right brain*, which is responsible for creative, impulsive, often outlandish thoughts and ideas, in order to generate an endless supply of one-of-a-kind ways to *show* a man how you feel about him in a way that's totally unexpected and unique to *him*. These types of actions are far more powerful than simply telling him.

Whether you're looking to make a great first impression, to hit a home run on your first or second date, to take your relationship to the next level, or to reward your boyfriend (or husband) for being amazing, Creative Seduction (also known as "Right-Brain Romance") is a crucial skill to have in your dating and relationship arsenal.

Note: If you disapprove of the label "seduction," realize it basically means the same thing as "romance"—one simply comes across as more "masculine" (stronger) and the other as more "feminine" (softer). You can use them interchangeably as you please.

As you master this five-step formula, your man will light up like a firecracker, brag to his friends about you, and quite possibly fall head-over-heels in love with you. As long as you two are together, he will smile more, complain less, cook dinner for you while you watch your favorite TV show, and in general, love you like no other man ever has, because you will make him feel like no other woman ever has. When this happens, sparks fly, hearts are won, wedding bells ring, and everyone wins. But it's up to you (and him) to escape the routine dating matrix and make it take place.

The 5-Step Formula

Step 1: Do Your Research

The idea here is to learn as much as you can about a man you're really into, *in preparation for* a future opportunity to go from, "I really think this man is cool," to "Wow! Did that really just happen? I think he could be 'the one.'"

Note: This first step is a continuation of the Awareness Approach in Chapter 6.

As you two are getting to know each other—whether you "met" online and have been texting and talking for a few weeks, crossed paths in a coffee shop, or you're on your first or second official date—you will naturally begin to create a *general* profile in your mind (or on paper) about who he is and what he's all about.

What kind of clothing does he usually wear? Is he preppy, outdoorsy, or buttoned up most of the time? Use the insights you gather to make educated guesses about his lifestyle and possible date ideas. For example, if he seems outdoorsy and laid-back, great date ideas might include a picnic at the local park or hiking.

How's his attitude and overall confidence? Is he upbeat, flashy, or hip? If so, maybe he'd love for you to step up your game and surprise him with a spontaneous evening learning to Salsa dance together at a local Latin dance club. If he's shy, that's probably not such a great date idea.

What else does his vibe or body language reveal about his personality? Does he ever up the ante when you flirt with him, practically daring you to mess with him even harder? Perhaps he'd love to know what's *really* on your mind in a salacious text message. If he is more introverted and rarely speaks his mind, that sort of thing might make him uncomfortable. But it might be worth a try anyway, starting with baby steps.

Ask him questions here and there like:

- What are your top three movies of all time?
- Which genre of music lights you up or makes you nostalgic?
- What's your favorite dessert? Why? What do you love about it?
- If you could go anywhere in the world, where would you go? Why?
- What sort of things do you think about that you've never told a soul?

The point here is to get him talking about all kinds of different topics. Listen carefully to his responses and make mental notes of *key insights* he reveals about himself and the inner workings of his mind. Don't do anything that would make it obvious to him that you're "studying" his every move, though this is exactly what you'll be doing. Strive to do it in a way that seems natural, like you're just curious and want to know all about him. That shouldn't be too hard because you most definitely want to know all about the man you are dating.

Step 2: Make a List of Unique Insights You Learn About Him

Capture and retain as many details about him as you can, the more unique they are to him, the better. For example, if he says his favorite beer is Miller Light, that's not very distinctive, so keep digging. If he says his favorite drink is "A Hole in One"—a mixed drink made with 1.5 ounces of Johnny Walker Red Label, 1 tablespoon of honey, 3 ounces unsweetened tea, and a lemon wedge—that's definitely worth remembering.

Put pen to paper or use the Notes app on your smart phone and record as many pertinent details as you can about the man who's courting you. Memorize them. The last thing you want to do is forget them, or to have to look them up in the heat of the moment.

Step 3: Give Your Brain a Break

Here's the tricky part. Every once in a while, you will want to stop thinking about the man in your life altogether—no future date ideas, no upcoming birthdays or anniversaries, nothing. Better yet, cease with mental activities altogether and go for a run, watch a movie, take a nap, run some errands, or play with your kids or your pet. The idea here is to take your mind completely off of him and his various interests or possible needs, wants, and desires. Be patient and wait for your *right brain* to kick in through this process and start generating random ideas. It knows what to do, given the right environment.

Step 4: Connect the Dots

Eventually, often when you least expect it, a little voice in your head will begin churning out a bunch of ways you could apply the insights you learned in steps one and two, such as:

- Texting each other or talking on the phone at night
- While on a first, second, or third date

- A creative birthday gift idea
- A random act of kindness
- A steamy love letter you could write and send to him
- An innovative way to romance your man

For example, if a man you're seeing revealed that he's a huge fan of the Chicago Cubs baseball team, loves local draft beers, and thinks women look hot in jerseys, you'd knock your next date out of the park if you connected the dots and told him when to pick you up, and what to wear, but didn't tell him where you two were going. That night, when he rings your doorbell, you're wearing cute shorts and a Cubs jersey, and you surprise him with two tickets to the Cubs game. On the way to the game, you tell him the name of a sports bar where they serve the best local draft beers. The plan is to go there before or after the game.

That's a straightforward example of putting all the pieces together.

Note: Many women don't get this far because they're used to sitting back and forcing the man to plan most of their dates. As you will see, taking the next step (step 5) and making a guy feel like the most fortunate man in the world because he's with you requires a little more imagination and confidence.

When your right brain starts churning out a bunch of random ways to *apply* the insights you learned about your love interest in steps one and two, filter out the mundane ideas and identify the one or two that get your adrenaline pumping. If you have a thought like, "I could *never* do that!" This is your left brain—your logical, rational self—kicking back in. **Ignore it.**

It might take you a week or more to complete these first four steps. The more you practice, the faster you'll get. Soon you won't even have to think about tapping into your right brain and you'll be able to use it on the fly, a great skill to have when flirting and being witty.

Step 5: Take Bold Action

Once you have your breakthrough idea, you'll use your *left brain* to work out the logistics and, if need be, to plan ahead. Will you be cooking dinner at his place? Watching a movie at your place? Enjoying a picnic at the park? Do you need to pick up a six-pack of his favorite beer? Should you put together a tantalizing playlist and place candles strategically throughout your home before he picks you up, so you're ready to rock when he drops you off at the end of the night and you invite him in for a nightcap? How will you go above and beyond to make the occasion special? *Trust your gut and make it happen.*

Two Real-Life "Case Studies"

Right-Brain Romance

In my first serious relationship—I was twenty—I met (and later fell in love with) the youngest daughter of a European diplomat. She was staying with her parents in Atlanta for the summer, then returning to her studies at the University of Paris, in France.

When she learned I went to a college in Texas, and heard me listening to a Garth Brooks CD, *The Hits* album, she started referring to me as her real-life American cowboy, and said we should go line dancing sometime. Those were a few of the *key insights* I learned by following steps 1–3 above. Here's how I implemented steps 4 and 5 a few weeks after meeting each other.

Late one summer evening while driving Sophie home from a dinner date, a breakthrough idea popped into my head. Instead of going straight home, I made of spur-of-the moment decision to take a slight detour and I drove us to a secluded, but well-lit parking lot between two baseball fields where I grew up playing ball.

When we arrived at a dead-end, I put the car in park and turned off the engine, but left the key in the ignition to keep the power on. Next, I got out of my Toyota 4-Runner, walked over and opened her door, took her by the hand, and escorted her toward the back of my vehicle.

Quickly, I hopped back into the driver's seat, rolled down the back window, slipped Garth Brooks' *The Hits* album into the CD player and turned it to track six, "The Dance"—Sophie's favorite— and turned up the volume.

I returned to the back of my truck, looked her in the eyes and asked her to dance. That night, while slow dancing under the stars, Sophie and I fell in love. As fate would have it, I'd fallen for a girl that lived halfway around the world. We discussed the idea of getting married and agreed to write each other. But when the summer ended, we went our separate ways and both started dating new people shortly thereafter. However, I doubt either of us will ever forget "the dance we shared . . . beneath the stars above."

Creative Seduction

Jeremy and Naomi met at a cozy lounge in South Florida with dimmed lighting, sweet smelling candles, and sultry beats. He was sitting at the bar when she walked in, and their eyes met from across the room like heat-seeking missiles. Long story short, when the bar closed, they made out like teenagers in the parking lot.

A week later, while daydreaming about Naomi, Jeremy got a spur-of-the-moment idea and emailed her a steamy love letter fantasy about them sharing a hot shower and him washing her body from head to toe.

The following Friday night, after a candlelit dinner they prepared together at her house, Naomi excused herself from the table, but told him to stay put. The next thing he knew the bathwater was running, "Bump n' Grind" was playing on her surround sound, and she reappeared wearing nothing but a black towel. She looked

Jeremy in the eyes and said, "Meet me in the bathroom in five minutes."

When Jeremy entered the steamy candlelit bathroom, his eyes locked on the most beautiful sight he'd ever seen—his sensual new girlfriend chest deep in a whirlpool of bubbles. She commanded him to disrobe and join her. A minute or two later, while sitting across from each other and gazing into each other's eyes, Jeremy said, "You're too far away from me." What happened next? Use your imagination . . . then use it some more.

His bold decision to share his desires (the power of suggestion) gave Naomi the greenlight to reciprocate, and she took daring action.

Why "Creative Seduction" Is a Winning Formula

I could've taken Sophie line dancing. But slow dancing to Garth Brooks in a parking lot was way more thoughtful, romantic, and memorable. Likewise, Naomi could've called or texted Jeremy and said, "I got your email. That sounds amazing." But choosing to reciprocate in her own unique way was a thousand times more creative, seductive, and grandiose.

Everyone wants their significant others to plan creative ways to show them how they feel about them. Remember, chemistry and cravings are mostly emotional, not logical. So, do things that are more spontaneous, authentic, clever, and maybe even a bit risky.

Note: This same "formula" is used by advertising agencies to generate innovative ways to communicate otherwise ordinary marketing messages for their clients' brands, because doing so is far more effective and profitable than simply saying, "Hey, you, buy this product."

When you've just met a man you'd like to pursue a romantic connection with, come up with your own unique way to say, "I'm attracted to you." Revisit the conversation starters in Chapter 6. Many of these include resourceful ways to say and do otherwise ordinary things.

If you've already given him your number and scheduled a first date, come up with your own unique way to say, "I'm different than all the other women you've dated," which will make him feel what he needs to feel to bring his A game.

If you're on a date and don't have any special plans, and your right brain spits out an idea for a spontaneous seduction, feel free to deviate from your original non-plan and live in the moment. This is one of the biggest keys to a soul-stirring love life.

What if Valentine's Day is approaching? He might appreciate a card and an engraved money clip. But secretly, he's hoping you'll go one step further and blow him away with your own way of saying, "You are mine."

Whatever you want to communicate to a man, it's up to you to connect the dots and make it happen. Spring into action and show him.

He Loves the Chicago Cubs, Eh?

Using the same insights from the scenario in Step 4 earlier—he loves the Chicago Cubs, local draft beers, and women who wear jerseys—instead of buying him two tickets to the game, you complete this strategic "formula" and invite your guy to watch the Cubs game together at your place.

While he's busy watching the game, you excuse yourself to use the ladies' room and return wearing an authentic Chicago Cubs baseball jersey, and a pair of boy-shorts or a thong that matches his team's colors—and maybe even some eye black.

If you don't know what eye black is, look it up online. This level of detail is what separates the fully armed women from the girls.

Don't forget the six-pack of his favorite local beer. Pull a crazy stunt or two like this, and he's all yours.

Tip: If you ever buy a sports jersey, hat, or t-shirt of your man's favorite team for yourself, do *not* buy a pink girly version of it. Most men will find you far sexier in the real thing. Seeing his feminine-looking woman in "masculine" fan gear will drive him wild.

When it comes to relationships and romance, it's the little things that matter most to many guys, too. Any woman can look cute. But it takes a real catch of a woman to dig deep, learn what her man secretly craves, generate her own unique ways to communicate her feelings, take valiant action, and reap the rewards. *That's the power of Creative Seduction.*

And then, before you know it, you'll be having "the talk."

Chapter 10

FROM COMMITMENT TO "HE PUT A RING ON IT!"

"But despite their differences, they had one important
thing in common . . . they were crazy about each other."

—Duke (*The Notebook*, Nicolas Sparks)

There are no rules which state how long you should date before
making a commitment to be "official" or exclusive. It depends
on the man you're with and your goals for your relationship. But
traditionally, one to three months of going out and getting to know
each other is a solid timeframe to work with. Maybe up to six
months, but no more than that, in my opinion.

Ideally, you will have discussed your relationship goals back
when you first started dating, so the desire to further define your
interconnection shouldn't be a surprise.

Defining Your Relationship

When you're ready to have "the talk," there's no right or wrong
way to do it. It's a great opportunity to tell each other how you're
feeling, and to say that you want to be in an exclusive bond. But you

shouldn't skip this conversation simply because things seem to be going well.

Defining your relationship *is* important because if this conversation never takes place, and your connection status and long-term goals are merely assumed, it's always possible that one or both of you thinks it's more casual and may still be dating other people, or one person wants to be in a committed relationship but actually has no desire to ever get married. That can lead to misunderstandings, wasted time, heartache, and frustration later.

If your goal is to be in a monogamous, long-term relationship, but you have no interest in getting engaged or married, that's perfectly fine, as long as you are both on the same page. It's your life, so you're free to create the lifestyle you want. But most men and women desire a serious relationship with the goal of getting engaged and later married, so that's the kind of status we're going to focus on.

Back in the day, it was expected that the man asked for exclusivity first, or even formally asked you to be his girlfriend. But as times and courtship rules have changed, anyone can start the conversation. If you've been dating a few months, you know you like him and that he likes you, it can be as simple as, "Hey, we like each other. Let's be exclusive," and then begin introducing him to your friends as your boyfriend. It can also be a formal request over a romantic dinner at your favorite restaurant, or a spontaneous feeling one of you pops on the other at a moment's notice.

Tip: If you are uncertain about your relationship status and you ask him, "What are we?" Don't be surprised if he mirrors your uncertainty and says, "I don't know, what are we?" Be more leader-like and tell him what you want or ask him a yes or no question. For example, "I want to be your girlfriend," or "Will you be my boyfriend?"

The most important thing when defining your relationship status is that you're both serious and honest with each other. This is not always done in *one* conversation, but through a series of open and honest communications over time.

You should also discuss your boundaries: What are your deal breakers? What constitutes cheating to you? You should know your own non-negotiables and be able to communicate those with your partner so he is aware of your boundaries, knows your limits, and will hopefully respect and honor them.

Once you are in a committed, monogamous relationship, there are a few key principles that you (an alpha-dominant woman) and your beta-dominant man will want to be aware of, in order to keep your ongoing relationship healthy, happy, and strong.

Remember, the "best practices" taught in most dating and relationship (and marriage) books are, unfortunately, *reversed* for alpha women and beta men. So, I've realigned them for you below.

The 5 Love Languages

According to Gary Chapman, author of *The 5 Love Languages: The Secret to Love That Lasts*, different people have disparate preferences when it comes to giving and receiving love. The five love languages are:

1. **Words of Affirmation:** Building a man up by telling him you think he's smart, thoughtful, sexy, and creative.

2. **Quality Time:** Being together in the same room, talking and making eye contact, and actively listening to each other—as opposed to being in the same room, but one person is watching TV while the other reads a book, and essentially ignoring each other. That doesn't count.

3. **Gifts:** Buying your man a gift that shows him you were listening a few weeks prior when he said his watch was

broken, or making him a photo collage of the quality times you've spent together over the past few months.

4. **Acts of Service:** Cleaning his apartment, organizing his home office, giving him a foot massage, or some other action-oriented gift.

5. **Physical Touch:** Hugging, kissing, scratching his back with your fingernails, flirtatious butt grabbing, or making love to each other with reckless abandon.

How the 5 Love Languages Work

Chapman says we all have "emotional love tanks." When our love tanks are full, the relationship we're in is fulfilling, resulting in feelings of love, peace, and harmony. But when our emotional needs are *not* being met, we tend to lash out at each other, causing drama in an attempt to get our partner to change their ways and give us what we want and need.

All too often we don't even know what we want, or we don't want to have to tell our significant other what that is. We'd prefer they listen and anticipate our individual needs, wants and desires, and then spring into action accordingly. But hoping for change can easily turn into disappointment.

A better approach is to watch your partner's behavior toward you, and seek to identify which love languages *he* prefers to communicate in. Or simply take the love language quiz[52] together to determine what you each need and discuss this more carefully.

Most people do for their partner what they wish their partner would do for them. For example, if a woman makes a big deal out of her man's birthday and makes it a special day just for him and gets him the perfect present, these are great indicators that her love languages are quality time, gifts, and acts of service. She most likely wants him to make a big deal for her birthday and do special things that day, too. But this sort of indirect communication can be difficult to decode if either of you doesn't understand how the five love languages work.

If a man's primary love languages are quality time and physical touch, buying him gifts might not fill up his love tank. It's a nice gesture and hopefully he appreciates his partner's efforts. But without the physical closeness he craves first and foremost, it's just a matter of time before he becomes dissatisfied overall. She may not be completely happy either, because he gives her lots of quality time and physical touch, but rarely surprises her with thoughtful gifts and doesn't perform many acts of service—her primary love languages.

If you *don't* keep each other's emotional love tanks full, problems will arise and you two will likely fight or drift apart. One or both of you could be tempted to get your needs met by someone else—physically or emotionally—or break up, needlessly, and go your separate ways.

You and your partner really need to learn each other's preferred love languages, and then speak to each other in those languages, even if that's not one of your strengths. This is one of the biggest keys to keeping your union healthy and strong.

How You Each Prefer to Handle Stress and Conflict

Some degree of stress and conflict is unavoidable, but how you two choose to deal with this is very important. Sometimes you might merely need a little time alone to process a situation; or to enjoy a good meal and a glass of wine; or to take a power nap to recharge after an exhausting day; or to go for a run or a walk. Other times, you might want to talk things through with your partner and consider their advice and willingness to help.

When beta men are stressed out, they typically want to talk about their problems. If you're his significant other, he will likely want to confide in you. However, when a beta man shares a problem with you or vents about his day, he's typically *not* asking for your advice and recommended solutions. He just wants you to listen, tell him you understand, and empathize with him, his emotions, and his situation. Empathy is a tremendous diffuser of distressing emotions.

As an alpha woman, you typically don't like to talk about your problems unless you want advice. So, when a beta man talks about his problems, you may instinctually put on your problem-solving hat and suggest possible solutions. If you do this, you will most likely annoy him, and he may get triggered and react emotionally in a negative way. Then you may get triggered and also react in an unfavorable way. The next thing you know you're both pissed off and neither of you has any clue why.

As a general rule, when he shares his feelings, it's best to respond with empathy for his feelings and maybe expressing your own feelings. If he shares facts, respond with facts. If he shares his feelings and you respond with facts or solutions, from his perspective you invalidate his feelings, and it turns into a giant misinterpretation.

On the flip side, if you get stressed out or annoyed, you may tend to shut down and isolate yourself. You likely want to be left alone so you can process your feelings on your own. But your beta man may think something is wrong and engage with you. Because he likes to talk about his problems, he may assume you'll want to talk about yours, too. He might also wonder if you're upset with *him* and if so, he'll want to know why. Although he's trying to be caring and loving, it's possible that his actions will likely irritate you and drive you even deeper into a shell.

The solution is simple. Your man needs to know how you prefer to handle stress or conflict. If you shut down and disappear *without* communicating with him, he will likely come looking for you, or try to call or text you to figure out what's wrong. Instead, tell him you need to be alone, not to worry about you, and that you'll be back when you're ready.

Remember, neither of you is right nor wrong. You're just different. Learning how each of you best handles stress and conflict and working through it together is vital for a healthy relationship.

Face Your Irrational Fears Together

"Are you paralyzed with fear? That's a good sign. Fear is good. Like self-doubt, fear is an indicator. Fear tells us what we have to do."

—STEVEN PRESSFIELD

Everyone fears getting hurt. Falling off a mountain and dying is an example of a *rational* fear. A fear of public speaking or being afraid to strike up a conversation with a man you're interested in, are examples of *irrational* fears.

I have no way of knowing what your biggest fears and anxieties are. But based on my years of market research on alpha women—and dating lots of them—I'm guessing that opening up and communicating with a man in a vulnerable way may not be a natural strength or desire of yours. If that's true, it's likely due to you having more of a "male brain" in function. This brain-type functionality must go through a longer process to interpret emotional meaning; has a preference for serious, short, and direct communication; is less emotional and more logical; trends toward impatience; and often views "vulnerability" as weakness.

But just because you are uncomfortable doing something, it doesn't mean you won't want to at least strive to improve (and the same is true for men). If you choose *not* to face some of these types of fears or discomforts, you may be unknowingly contributing to persistent dating and relationship problems in your life.

Zig Ziglar, a renowned author and motivational speaker said, "F.E.A.R. has two meanings: Forget Everything And Run or Face Everything And Rise. The choice is yours." Which of these two acronyms best describes how you typically react when you're *uncomfortable* in a courtship context? If you want something you've never had before, you must do something you've never done before.

Paradoxically, fear often causes the very thing we dread the most to come true. For example, a fear of intimacy usually leads to a lack of intimacy. Fear of being cheated on, broken up with, or divorced leads to trust issues, which often lead to being cheated on, broken up with, or a divorce. Fear of getting hurt often leads to getting hurt. **We are here on the planet to *overcome!***

Love begins at the end of your comfort zone, so get used to being uncomfortable and lean into it. Action breaks the power of fear and builds confidence. Inaction breeds doubt and fear. So, face your fears head on and rise to the occasion.

> "Many of our fears are tissue-paper thin, and a single courageous step would carry us clear through them."
>
> —Brendan Francis

Don't let your current hesitations or previous relationship wounds dictate your future. Strive to date from a clean slate and love like you've never been hurt. Yes, you could still get hurt. But if you don't take any chances, then you don't win, either. Love attracts love, so endeavor to be as loving as you can.

Give Each Other the Best Versions of Yourselves

As an alpha woman in a relationship with a beta man, your degree of "masculine" energy has pros and cons. It's a big reason you may be strong, ambitious, disciplined, a ball buster (in a good way) sometimes, a fighter, and an adventurous lover.

But from the beta man's perspective, it can also make you seem a bit stiff and robotic, unemotional, and not nearly as energetically feminine—playful, spontaneous, and carefree—as he might like you to be sometimes.

As you know, you cannot change the essence of your being. But you can make a conscious effort to loosen up a little and act more energetically feminine, if you so desire, just as you may want your beta man to take life more seriously and be more energetically masculine.

Extreme alpha tendencies to watch out for include being overly controlling, domineering, listening poorly, communicating weakly, angering easily, demanding, unforgiving, and acting somewhat insensitive.

Beta men need, want, and desire your strength, encouragement, servant leadership, and love. Tough love and being a little bossy sometimes is fine, too, because many beta men need it and actually appreciate it. Just be aware of the tone you take and strive to make any "in your face" confrontations as constructive and loving as possible.

Being a Workaholic

As an alpha woman, again, your primary self-worth may come from being successful in your career. The beta man's primary self-worth may come from helping others, or helping you and being together. As a result, your relationship may be more important to him than his career, and your career, in many ways, may be more important to you than your relationship with him.

Additionally, his primary love languages will likely be quality time, physical touch, and words of affirmation. At least two of these require being together in person. If you're a workaholic, he should understand the pressure you feel and the satisfaction you get from being successful. But his desire to spend quality time with you is no less important, because relationships are a two-way street. (The same applies if *he* is a workaholic and you're not getting enough quality time.)

Do what you have to do workwise but try not to work so much that he never gets to spend quality time with you and feels neglected. Find a compromise that works well for both of you.

Case Study

In the movie *The Intern,* Anne Hathaway plays the character of "Jules," the founder and CEO of a blossoming Internet fashion site. Portrayed as a stereotypical extremely alpha woman, she works 80+ hours a week growing her business, which doesn't leave much time to spend with her stereotypical beta husband "Matt," and their daughter.

Predictably, she finds out her husband is cheating on her with another woman. She is irate and she feels extremely disrespected.

Her interpretation as to why he cheated is that her success makes him feel like his manhood is being threatened. He acted out because the new woman makes him feel more like a man. But in *my* opinion, the most likely scenario is that Matt acted out because—like many beta men—his primary love languages are quality time, physical touch, and words of affirmation, and these "emotional love tanks" were mostly empty (he felt unloved). The new woman gave him the time, attention, and affection he innately required. **I'm not making excuses for his conduct, merely analyzing it.**

I realize this is just a movie, but we've all heard several similar real-life stories about a "power wife" filing for a divorce from her "supporting man" because he cheated on her. Again, I'm *not* excusing his behavior, but there are two sides to every story and it's worth considering from all angles. I wouldn't be surprised if *some* pre-cheating beta husbands feel like their alpha wives are "cheating" on them with their careers.

Reactive versus Proactive Happiness

"Equanimity is neither apathy nor indifference: you are warmly engaged with the world but not troubled by it. Through nonreactivity, it creates a great space for compassion, loving-kindness, and joy at the good fortune of others."

—Rick Hanson, Ph.D.
with Richard Mendius, MD, *Buddha's Brain*

The best relationships are between two happy, balanced, and whole individuals. For most people, being happy and fulfilled requires proactively working to maintain control of their thoughts and emotions. One of the best ways to gain more self-control is to increase your self-awareness of common daily triggers. The biggest joy robbers for most people are the Internet and irritating people.

Instead of choosing to allow others to emotionally set you off, which is almost always in direct opposition to your personal joy, start practicing self-control (i.e., equanimity).[53] For example, if you see a news headline that irritates you, or a Facebook post you strongly disagree with, instead of reacting emotionally, acknowledge the feeling of being agitated, and then move on with your day. You're still reacting but you're doing so in a way which serves your highest and best interests, by not responding, choosing to, as they say, "let it go."

Rather than joining heated online debates and choosing to feel outraged, or simply clogging your precious headspace with things you have almost zero power to change, choose to focus on a pleasant memory, or an event you're looking forward to attending in a few days, or simply being thankful for your family and friends, and the many opportunities you have. The more you practice *not* allowing others to control your emotions, the stronger your self-control patterns will become. Soon the things that set most people off won't even faze you. You'll simply ignore them or acknowledge them and choose not to react. This learned skill of rising above it all can increase your daily happiness exponentially.

So how does this relate to your relationships? If you work 60-plus hours a week and are constantly on the run, you may have very little margin in your life. As a result of this lack of bandwidth, your boyfriend (or a man you meet online) could say something that rubs you the wrong way and boom—you're pissed off and have no interest in talking to him (or meeting him or dating him) anymore.

If this resonates with you, you might consider working less, or making time to relax and unwind a higher priority. If you're constantly on edge, you may be convinced the people who trigger you are the problem. In reality, you are the only person who can implement full emotional control.

A person who is easily angered isn't likely to be a good partner (or dater). So, as you increase your self-awareness and strive to be less reactive and more proactive about your personal happiness, this will absolutely spill over into your love life.

Love and Respect

Everyone wants both love and respect, but some people need or want one more than the other.

Dr. Emerson Eggerichs is an internationally known speaker on the topic of male-female relationships. He has authored several books including the national bestseller, *Love & Respect, The Love She Most Desires—The Respect He Desperately Needs*, published in 2004, which is a Platinum and Book of the Year award winner, selling over 1.6 million copies. This book is also commonly referred to as "The Relationship Bible" by licensed professional Christian counselors.

Eggerichs' big idea is that most women desire love first and foremost, and men need respect first and foremost. That may be true for some men and women, but like most dating and relationship (and marriage) books, it too is based on the simplistic alpha man–beta woman paradigm.

Note: In my opinion, Dr. Eggerichs is almost certainly a beta-dominant man.

It's possible many alpha women *believe* love is their primary desire, and that many beta men *believe* respect is their primary need, because that's what you've both been indoctrinated to accept. But the opposite could be more accurate: you may actually desire to be respected more than you want to be loved. Most beta men crave love more than they want to be respected.

The best way to discern which is most important to you is to ask yourself which of these emotions tee you off the most when you feel like you're *not* getting it. Does feeling unloved really set you off? Or does feeling disrespected make your blood boil? My guess is when you feel disrespected, you will instinctively react somewhat unlovingly. When beta men feel unloved, they often react in a disrespectful manner.

The ultimate key is balancing you and your partner's individual needs for both love and respect. When a person feels loved they typically respond lovingly, and when they feel respected they show respect to others accordingly.

Love and Respect Trigger Languages

Your respective triggers will typically be the *opposite* of your primary love/respect languages. For example:

Love/Respect Language	Triggers
Words of Affirmation	Silence, criticism, nagging, disregarding one's opinion
Quality Time	Not enough quality time, not the kind one needs/desires
Gifts	Not receiving any, not enough, not the type one cherishes
Acts of Service	Not appreciative, not helpful, lazy, disorderly
Physical Touch	No physical touch, not enough, not the type one craves

Remedies

If you feel disrespected, tell him why, what he can do differently, and, in turn, give him the kind of *love* he most desires. If you bury your feelings and don't communicate with him, or you retaliate and make him feel unloved, you're probably going to cause *both* of you to feel even more pain and frustration.

If he feels unloved, he needs to speak up and tell you why, including specific things he believes you can do to improve, and correspondingly give you the kind of *respect or love* you desire most.

If he doesn't do this, his actions or inactions are likely to be equally counterproductive.

You can also both strive to be less reactive by acknowledging a feeling of being triggered by your partner and then just letting it go. Giving each other the benefit of the doubt is also a powerful choice. For example, did he *intend* to disrespect you? Is it possible he was being his normal self and you *interpreted* what he said, did, or didn't do as disrespectful, because work is stressful and you are more on edge than usual? Or did he *misinterpret* what you said, did, or didn't do as being unloving because he's feeling overwhelmed by life or being overly sensitive? Are you two in completely different brain states? (You logical, him emotional, or vice versa.)

Remind each other of your numerous potential differences, forgive each other, and strive to be more proactive in your efforts to love and respect each other for your mutual benefit as a happy and healthy power couple.

Weekly Partner "Pow-Wows"

"Communication is lubrication."

—LAURYN EVARTS AND MICHAEL BOSSTICK,
THE SKINNY CONFIDENTIAL HIM & HER PODCAST

I highly recommend scheduling a weekly check-in with your partner to see how you're both doing and, if need be, to course correct before a small issue turns into a much bigger one. Keeping your communication lines open and active is crucial.

Pick a time to get together each week, maybe Sunday evenings at 8 pm, and make sure your relationship is on the right track. If it's not, dialogue with each other. Here are a few questions to consider asking each other:

1. How are you feeling?
2. Why do you feel this way?
3. What do you want more of?
4. What are you afraid of?
5. Is there anything bothering you?

Don't let each other off the hook with one-word answers. Go a little deeper if you sense your partner isn't being totally honest or forthcoming with you. It's better to do a little maintenance each week than to let something slip through the cracks and become a much bigger issue.

One week your pow-wow might be ten minutes and filled with nothing but pleasant memories, high-fives, and hugs and kisses. Another session might take two hours and get a little heated at times. As long as you're open and honest with each other, there's no right or wrong way to do this. As your alliance progresses, you may switch these to monthly check-ins, but I do not suggest ever stopping them completely.

Speaking of pow-wows, it's important to keep the chemistry in your relationship alive and well. So, here are six ways to reward your man for being a badass and co-create more "pow-*wows!*"

6 Ways to Romance His Pants Off

If you're not a natural romantic or seductress, learning to be more creative with romance, foreplay, and seducing your man will pay huge dividends. In fact, being his best lover ever could be the key to his undying love and lifelong loyalty. Being an average lover could also be a deal breaker for him—and the same could be true for you.

Here are six ways to be more proactive and captivate your man.

1. Candles

Whether enjoying a romantic home-cooked dinner, preparing a hot bath for two, or gearing up for an evening of kissing and love making, lighting candles is an easy way to set the mood.

2. Romantic or Seductive Music

Usher, Marvin Gaye, Whitney Houston, Shakira, the *Fifty Shades of Grey* Soundtrack—whatever puts you in the mood—create a playlist on Spotify or iTunes so it's ready to go at a moment's notice.

3. Massage Oils

A strategically timed neck and shoulder massage for him, or asking him to give you a foot and leg massage can easily lead to releasing more than just muscle tension.

4. Sensual Lingerie

Many women go to great lengths to look sexy or beautiful in public, but drop the ball when it comes to dressing provocatively for their man in the bedroom. Don't be one of them.

Wearing lingerie *you* are confident in and *he* finds sexy is key. Different men prefer different looks. So, throw him a copy of your preferred lingerie catalog and a pen and tell him to start circling; or take him shopping with you and pull him into your dressing room; or do some shopping on your own and surprise him.

Many beta men love surprises, and get as much satisfaction from the buildup as the main event, because mental arousal may be their primary kick starter. So, consider disappearing to use the ladies' room and reappearing wearing something not so lady-like.

Seeing you in a silk teddy, a push-up bra with matching undies, or a lusty garter dress with thigh-highs will light him up like the sky on the Fourth of July. Once his "fuse" is lit, brace yourself for an explosive evening.

Tip: Halloween may only come around once a year, but "spell-binding" costumes can be purchased online and worn year-round.

5. Intimate Communication

Many beta men love communication, especially intimate communication, so whatever you're thinking and feeling in the heat of the moment (during sex or foreplay), you should seriously consider sharing with your man. Remember, beta men aim to please. And the best way to let him know he's pleasing you is to both show and tell him. Remove your filter and speak your mind.

It's also important to communicate your needs, wants, and desires. For example, if you're making love in one position and you'd like to feel him a different way, just be honest and say so.

> "A lot of people are afraid to say what they want.
> That's why they don't get what they want."
>
> —MADONNA

6. Imagination + Bold Action

From dirty talk to role playing, as long as you're both up for it, the only limit is your imagination and your willingness to take bold action.

If you're in the mood to pleasure your man in a specific manner, you could tell him what you want to do. But it's far sexier to spring into action and show him. Ideally, your man will make an effort to practice "Sexual Chivalry"—ladies, first.

Note: I'm fully aware you likely want *him* to be the "Alpha" and spring into action, but beta men love alpha women, *not* beta women. Take more risks and see how he reacts. If you don't get a strong enough reaction, strengthen your appeal. Many beta men are amazing lovers because they want you to enjoy it as much as they do. If your man is not a masterful lover, or at least has room for improvement, and you don't want to have to *tell* him exactly what you want him to do, you can hire me to coach him and I will "man him up" for you. (That goes for any other skill in this book, too.)

Again, I'm not suggesting you have to do any of these things specifically. But you shouldn't shy away from opportunities to show your man your sensual side just because society taught you that's not appropriate behavior for a "sweet princess" like you. He may love for you to take the lead, share a fantasy, initiate physical contact, and lead him to lead you.

You're the alpha, queen of the jungle, so do your thing!

The best love life is about far more than just the physical act of being together. It's about the anticipation; the teasing and touching; flirting and laughing; opening up and communicating your needs, wants, and desires with each other; and fulfilling them for your mutual pleasure and satisfaction.

When play time is over, go back to being the respectable woman he loves and adores. The polarity between you acting like a "good girl" and a "bad girl" will drive him crazy in a good way, and help ensure he continues to treat you with respect and loving kindness.

And remember, when it comes to "misbehaving," everyone has their *own* personal values and desired timeline. So, take these tips in that light and apply them whenever or however you and your man agree on.

Nailing Special Occasions

As a relatively new couple in a committed relationship, special occasions can be a double-edged sword. If you're on the same page and you meet or exceed each other's celebratory expectations, your relationship will grow stronger and your love for each other deeper.

However, if you're not of the same mind in this matter, and one of you doesn't meet or exceed the other's expectations, special occasions can be the kiss of death. That's why it's important to discuss your personal or family traditions, and what each holiday means to you.

The main holidays for most couples are:

> Birthdays
>
> Anniversaries
>
> Valentine's Day
>
> Thanksgiving
>
> Christmas, Hanukkah, Kwanzaa
>
> New Year's Eve

Some people don't care about Valentine's Day, and some people have huge expectations. Same with birthdays and anniversaries. Communication is extremely important in discussing which holidays and occasions are of key significance to each person.

Gifts

If you are expecting a big gift and he gets stressed out trying to pick one, or doesn't think your six-month anniversary is a big thing, one or both of you is going to be disappointed. And this can lead to smoldering resentment.

Valentine's Day is Eric's favorite *and* least favorite holiday because he's a natural romantic, but he also knows expectations can be sky high. And he's been through two different breakups the day after Valentine's Day. One memory stands out in particular.

A few years ago, he met a girl he really liked three weeks before the big day, but he wasn't sure how to play it since they'd just met.

He decided to go big anyway and prepared a romantic candlelit steak dinner with a bottle of her favorite red wine; and gave her a handwritten card and two-dozen roses. She wasn't sure what would be appropriate either, and didn't even get him a card. They dated anyway, but the following year *she* went all out and *he* hardly did anything. They broke up the next day.

Two years later, he told his new girlfriend the level of thought he typically puts into Valentine's Day gifts, and that it would mean the world to him if she did, too. What happened next? She invited him over to her place for dinner. When he arrived the lights were off and candles were lit; she was wearing a come-hither red dress; and she gave him her present—fifty-two pieces of hand-cut cardboard sewn together into a "card-deck" scrapbook. The front read, *52 Reasons I'm in Love with You.* Each card showcased her favorite memories from their nine months dating—photos as a couple; handwritten love notes; movie ticket stubs she saved from the night she dragged him to the premiere of *Magic Mike*; and so on.

Eric chose to be open and honest with her about the sort of gift that would make his heart melt and gave her the insights she needed to reciprocate. She hit a grand slam home run.

3-Step Gift-Giving Formula

If you really like a guy and want to make sure you nail every special occasion, here's my three-step gift-giving formula. (To be clear, I'm suggesting you do all three on big holidays.)

1. Get him a card and hand-write something thoughtful in it.
2. Buy him a physical gift like a watch, Amazon Echo Spot, or fishing gear.
3. Make him a gift from the heart, such as a framed picture of you two, or write him a poem.

Ideally, he will reciprocate. For example, on your one-year anniversary, he might give you a bouquet of red roses (or a Love Is Art kit), a piece of jewelry, and a handwritten card. If he doesn't, or you don't want to take that chance, feel free to share my formula with him or tell him what you want.

Wowing His Friends and Family

If you have a tight group of friends, you'll likely want their seal of approval about your new man, especially if you think he could be "the one." The same will likely be true for his friends, and more importantly, his parents and siblings, if applicable. Making a good impression with his buddies shouldn't be too difficult. It can be as simple as looking put together and being polite, and you should be golden. If he and his friends are jokesters or sports fanatics, telling a joke or being able to hold your own in a sports conversation should help win them over.

But unlike his pals, who can come and go, the biggest deal is making a great impression on his parents. When invited to meet his folks at their home, for example, bringing flowers or some sweets is never a bad idea. But the real gift is you—your smile, your energy, and your feelings about their son. You may be tempted to keep to yourself a little more than usual while meeting his family. But I encourage you to be yourself, too.

Parents want to see why their son is so crazy about you, so show them. Ask them questions about him, like what was he like as a teenager? Asking to see baby pictures and oohing and ahhing over them can be a great way to embarrass him while sharing a few laughs with his parents. This is a great way to bond with his family because it shows you're comfortable being one of them.

Minor public displays of affection are encouraged, too. Whether sitting next to your boyfriend or going for an evening walk with him and his parents, holding your guy's hand and wanting to be physically close with him will warm his parents' hearts and show them why he feels fortunate to have you in his life. What most parents truly care about is seeing their son (or daughter) truly happy, loved, and cared for.

Meeting each other's families should also be fun. If his parents ask you if you have any preferences, such as which board game you'd like to play or what you'd like for dinner, don't be shy. Speak up and give them the opportunity to make you happy. You are their guest, after all. If they don't ask if you have a preference, be polite and go with the flow.

Note: For major family holidays like Thanksgiving and Christmas, it's a good idea to discuss who's going where and if the other person is invited. For example, if you two live in California, his parents live in Michigan and your parents are in New York, and one or both of you were hoping to spend the holidays together, feelings can get hurt if one person says they're spending Christmas with their family and doesn't even bother to ask the other person what their plans are. Yes, this could depend on how long you two have been dating. But to be on the safe side, talk to each other. Assumptions will get you two into trouble more often than not.

If his siblings are present, interact with them. If they happen to have kids (his nieces or nephews), playing with them is a great way to show you care. It's not rocket science. Just interact with everyone you meet, have fun, and be yourself.

Whenever I've brought home a serious girlfriend, my mom asked me ahead of time what my girlfriend likes to eat and drink. This way she could go grocery shopping and prepare special treats to welcome her. My parents also plan activities she will enjoy. Taking a girlfriend home with me is a special occasion because I know she will be treated like royalty. This gives me confidence and peace of mind about introducing them to my family.

If your parents are like mine, that's awesome. If not, and you really want the occasion to go well, you might consider coaching your parents in this matter. If your man loves to grill steaks, maybe ask your dad to grill steaks for dinner one evening. If he loves grilled salmon, grill that.

Also, manage expectations for what your boyfriend can expect, and what you want him to do. For example, your father may ask him to say a blessing before dinner, so he should be prepared for that possibility. Or it may mean the world to your mom if he cleared the table and helped her with the dishes.

In summary, a great relationship doesn't happen by accident. It requires hard work, being thoughtful, and striving to make everyone happy. This includes making a good impression with each other's families. If you get married, you join their tribe and they join yours.

Pre-Engagement and Engagement Prep

Before taking the next step, there are a few big issues you two should probably discuss, such as how each of you handles finances, what is your philosophy regarding big purchases and savings, and whether or not you want children. You should be able to be open about your wants and needs in a potential marriage, and he will want to be able to, also.

Timelines for big life steps like getting married, buying a home, and having kids are also important to discuss in depth and be honest about. If you want to get married in two years, but your partner is thinking he won't be ready for four years, that's something you should clearly know about each other.

Getting engaged should never be a total surprise. A proposal— the act of him getting down on one knee and asking you to marry him—can be, but the engagement itself should not. You would've at least joked about getting married by now or talked about a future together.

Once you're both on the same page, you can begin to lead him to take steps toward an engagement by reading bridal magazines like *Wedding Style* and *Destination Weddings & Honeymoons,* or an engagement ring catalog while he's watching TV, and show him photos of rings you like instead of asking every week when he is going to propose. Give him space, too.

Most women want to be surprised by their man's proposal. If you hate surprises or desire a little more control as to how it plays out, discuss the type of proposal you're both comfortable with.

A proposal can be, but doesn't have to be, a grand romantic gesture. There's no right or wrong way to do it, but you should absolutely be in agreement regarding what you want in your marriage and in the future in general. If it's important to you for your partner to ask for your father's blessing, make this clear to him. He's not a mind reader and we are all different. Talk about it and communicate what you want and need.

> "So it's not gonna be easy. It's going to be really hard; we're gonna have to work at this every day, but I want to do that because I want all of you. I want all of you, forever, every day. You and me . . . every day."
>
> —Noah (*The Notebook*, Nicholas Sparks)

A Day You'll Remember for the Rest of Your Life

Ideally, your man will use something like my 5-step "Right-Brain Romance" formula to strategize, develop, and execute a special proposal that will be unique to your relationship. For example, he might create a scavenger-hunt-like trail of numbered love notes for you to find and read. Each note will end with a clue about where to find the next one. Maybe the last clue leads you into your closet—it's taped to a new dress he bought for you to wear on this special day. The note says: "Put this on and meet me by the river where we shared our first kiss."

When you arrive, he pays you a bold compliment that makes you blush, and starts to tell you the many reasons he's incredibly thankful to have you in his life.

Before you know it, the moment you've been *co-creating* is here. He takes you by the hand, gets down on one knee, looks up and into your eyes and says something like, "You're the best thing that's ever happened to me, and I don't want to spend another second on this planet without you."

He pulls a felt ring box out of his pocket, opens it, and asks you, "Will you make me the happiest man in the world and marry me?"

You'll say, "Yes! Oh my gosh, yes!"

He'll slide the gorgeous engagement ring onto your finger; then stand up, wrap his arms around you, and kiss you like there's no tomorrow.

A crowd of people you didn't know were watching you will clap their hands and let out a roar. You'll look over and realize they are your parents and his, and a few of your closest friends. He arranged for them to fly in from across the country to share this moment with you two.

A videographer is filming the whole thing, too.

Two servers wearing tuxedo-jackets will appear out of nowhere holding bottles of your favorite champagne, and pour everyone a glass.

Just when you're thinking, *This day couldn't possibly get any better*, your fiancé will put two fingers in his mouth and whistle as loud as he can.

A valiant white horse will come running toward you two; you'll both hop on; and you'll ride off into the sunset together.

Or kick this fairytale to the curb and write your *own* happily ever after.

"Don't follow the crowd, let the crowd follow you."

—MARGARET THATCHER

Success Story

The following is all feedback from an anonymous client—in her own words—before, during, and after completing my original *Get The Guy You Want* coaching program (now this book):

Before working together:

I'm 57 years old and have been widowed going on 8 years (that's a good portion of my pain). I was successfully married for 28 years to the love of my life. I just started dating about 3 years ago. In that time, I've had only one serious relationship (engaged), but learned the man I was engaged to was still active on the dating apps/sites (nice, huh?). It obviously didn't end well.

My dating efforts have yielded no real connections, either, because I get bored with the men I meet super-fast, the men end up being totally inappropriate, or the ones I like are just not into me (the other pain point). I guess I should mention that I've been on a lot of first dates, but very few second dates.

Halfway through the program:

Wow! Who else besides me had an epiphany? I thought this handsome, hot, successful alpha man that I've been seeing was just not that into me. It seemed like it always just fizzled between us and never really went anywhere, in spite of the intellectual, emotional, and physical attraction and compatibility we share. Only to discover that in reality, he's a shy beta and all I needed to do was be more assertive with him. In his case I had to stick a pin in his butt! Some may need a cattle prod.

He said he loves a woman who has no qualms about being in control and prefers it. Who knew?

Her long-held beliefs about her late husband shifted too:

Double wow! The deeper we go into the program, the more I realize my late husband was beta-dominant with alpha traits. There is such a misconception that beta males are not masculine. My husband was a man's man whose personality was larger than life. He hunted, fished, played competitive sports, power lifted, coached little league football, etc. He also did all of the cooking, carpooling, cared for our sons—basically did all of the things a wife and mother is supposed to do according to society while I was traveling and building my career.

I used to catch hell from a lot of people about my decisions to pursue my career goals rather than staying home and being a mommy. In most aspects our roles were reversed. However, he wasn't needy, clingy, or overly romantic or affectionate, and all of the other negative misconceptions with which beta males are labeled.

Initially, he was much less ambitious than I preferred, but with encouragement and support, he built a very successful business, as well. With all of that said, it worked for us. It was all about balance.

Her overall program experience, and her results:

I went into the program with an open mind, but with a bit of trepidation with thoughts of "What makes this program so different from the others that were unsuccessful for me?"

Scott's program resonated with me, as I've always approached dating in a different manner than the rest of my single friends, and it validated what came so naturally to me. I was reluctant to follow my instincts because they didn't align with how I had been taught a woman was supposed to approach and behave during the courtship phase of a relationship.

In all honesty, had I gone through Scott's program when I first starting dating 3 years ago, I wouldn't have had to go through numerous first dates and a failed engagement. Scott knows his stuff and I'm so happy he chose me to participate in the program!

I've read all the self-help books from the "dating gurus" with PhDs and other letters after their names, and they were all the same and not one of them applicable to me. It was as if they had the roles in reverse and none of their advice helped me a bit. Throughout Scott's program I had several "Aha Moments" that I never had with any of the others.

Prior to participating in the program, I had resigned myself to the fact that I would probably never, ever find a love like I had with my late husband, and would most likely die a single (widowed) woman—not an outlook anyone wants for themselves. But it was my reality at the time.

During the program, I found myself opening up to men that I would have not otherwise considered as a potential partner for me. As I grew in my enlightenment as result of the program, so did my "dance card." It was as if a whole other world opened for me and I had my pick of men wanting to spend time with me and be in a committed relationship. I was like holy shit, Scott, where were you and your program three years ago when I first started dating again?

Since I completed the program, I've found a wonderful man who loves me unconditionally. We're crazy about each other and wedding bells will be ringing loud and clear in the very near future. To say I'm ecstatic is truly an understatement. Had it not been for the Get the Guy You Want program, I would probably still be looking at a bleak romantic future.

Thank you, Scott!

Months later she told me:

I have never been so happy and in love as I am now. He makes me want to be softer and more gentle and I love that. If I hadn't encouraged him to pursue me, he wouldn't have.

She Went From "Dating Sucks" to "We're in Love!" Faster and Easier. Now It's Your Turn!

As an alpha woman, you are a natural born leader. That is your identity, your duty, and your destiny. The time has come for you to step up and lead like you've never led before *in the dating world.*

When word gets out about this book, and millions of women realize the kind of power they've been unknowingly giving up all these years, I predict the dating world will be turned upside down, and a feeding frenzy could very well ensue. Some women may go on a dating spree and have lots of fun. Others will get serious immediately, and meet and keep an amazing beta man faster and easier than they ever thought possible.

If you decide to hold out a little longer, and continue to *pretend* you're a passive beta woman who needs a man to rescue you, you could miss out on dating and potentially marrying an incredible beta man—because another woman might beat you to the punch.

Remember, dating is competitive. The goal is to differentiate yourself in desirable ways and add value to a man's life starting the instant you two connect.

I strongly advise you to change your traditional "stories" and your love life by doing what is right, not what is easy. Pivoting isn't always easy, but it is necessary!

That means no more waiting for beta men to make the first move, or to message you first, or to ask you out, or to plan and pay for your dates. Take back your personal power, be the badass woman you've always been, and use this *New Dating Playbook* to achieve your relationship goals faster and easier.

How to Protect Your New Dating and Relationship Paradigm (And Overall Worldview)

Now that you know the truth about alpha women and beta men (and balanced people), be on the lookout for pop culture, media, movies, Internet memes, "experts," and uninformed men's and women's *beliefs* that are either flat-out untrue, or simply do not apply to you. For example:

1. "Men: If you can't control your woman, you've found a good one."

That may be true. But beta men are the wild ones because they have far more "feminine" energy than an alpha woman. It would be much more accurate to say, "Women: If you can't control your man, you've found a good one."

2. "When a man loves a woman, she becomes his weakness. When a woman truly loves a man, he becomes her strength. This is called the exchange of power."

It *could* be more accurate to say, "When an alpha woman loves a beta man, he becomes her weakness. When a beta man truly loves an alpha woman, she becomes his strength. This is called the exchange of power."

3. "Every man wants an alpha woman until they learn what it takes to keep one."

Again, if an alpha woman expects a beta man to match her at her greatest strengths, her unrealistic expectations are the primary problem, not his inability to do so for countless reasons we've already discussed. The same is true if a beta man expects an alpha woman to match him at his greatest strengths. But together they can meet each other halfway and end up more whole.

4. "A gentleman knows what he wants and goes after it. It's in his biology to do so. If he is not coming after you ladies, he does NOT want you. No exceptions."

Again, this is only *innately* true for the highest level of alpha men—less than 5% of the male population.

It could also be true for *you*. "An alpha woman knows what she wants and goes after it. It's in her biology to do so."

In summary, don't believe everything you hear. Protect your newly discovered gender insights and you will be a lot more successful in life and love.

Beware of Traditional Dating and Relationship (And Marriage) "Experts"

The typical dating and relationship (or marriage) advisor—whether they are a PhD, a licensed professional counselor, or some other title—seldom takes your dominant energy or brain type into consideration. You are merely a "woman" (or a "man") to them as they plug you into their *learned or assumed* gender stereotypes and simplistic remedies. It is quite likely they cannot even identify their *own* dominant energy or brain type. How can this "expert" possibly give you (and/or your partner) an accurate psychological evaluation?

The most likely scenario is that many beta male PhDs and other professionals, who probably don't realize they are betas, are advising other beta men as though they were alphas, and advising alpha women as though they were betas—and vice versa for many alpha women PhDs, LPCs, and other relationship (and marriage) professionals. If you think about this for a moment or so, you will clearly see the absurdity of this reality, or at least get a good belly laugh.

Furthermore, in my opinion, the vast majority of people in the dating services industry—authors, dating and relationship coaches, matchmakers, online dating company founders—appear to be either an alpha-dominant woman or a beta-dominant man, often to an extreme degree.

Therefore, if you catch anyone giving you love advice based on the simplistic alpha man-beta woman paradigm; or using "masculine energy" to refer to *all* men, and "feminine energy" to refer to *all* women; or they can't credibly decipher who is which type, you should probably run! Or, at the very least, realize they might not be fully qualified to help you make the best dating and relationship decisions *for you*.

Note: There *are* PhDs, LPCs, coaches, and matchmakers who are equally committed to researching, developing, and sharing innovative and progressive gender psychology insights. Subscribe to my email list to learn about collaborations with *enlightened* relationship experts I know and trust.

Dating and Relationship Coaching

If you are interested in working with me one-on-one, in a group coaching format, or attending one of my events, visit my website: NewDatingPlaybook.com and join my email list to learn about my latest product and service offerings.

Learn or Confirm Your Degree of "Alpha" and Receive Custom Coaching

The best way to learn or confirm your degree of "alpha" sexual essence (i.e. brain type) is to hire me to analyze you *personally*—via Skype, or in my Facebook Group Coaching Program—because self-testing quizzes, in this book and elsewhere, are susceptible to one's individual biases and socially programmed gender psychology influences. For example, as an alpha woman, you might *believe:*

- "I'm naturally intuitive because I'm a woman." (Based on the phrase, women's intuition)

- "I'm more emotional than men because I'm a woman."

- "I'm a nurturer because females are more nurturing than males."

Maybe you are and maybe you aren't. These qualities are also relative, meaning it matters whether you are more nurturing or less nurturing, for example, *compared to* other women and the typical beta man. Also, it's you—your eyes, your facial expressions, your body type, and so on—that matters most, not necessarily how you answer a quiz.

There are many variables in this equation, and this can all be very confusing, which can easily lead to inaccurate self-testing. The fastest and easiest way I know for you to get the most accurate assessment is to work with me, so I can analyze you personally, and advise you accordingly. Remember, your degree of alpha essence *also* affects the degree of beta man you will most likely attract, which could impact how you approach dating.

Note: If you are in a relationship (or married), I'm also available to "Train Your Man" regarding the skills in this book, and beyond. I will even fly to your location for private lessons.

I Need Your Help to Make
My "Fairytale" Come True, Too

Have you ever seen the movie *Jerry Maguire* starring Tom Cruise? If so, you might remember the scene where "Jerry" wakes up in the middle of the night with an epiphany about his place in the world, and spends the next twelve hours writing his "Mission Statement."

When I was a junior in high school, I woke up in the middle of the night with a convincing premonition about *my* future place in the world. I raced up the stairs to my parent's bedroom, *wisely* knocked on their door, woke them up, and said:

"Mom! Dad! I figured out what I want to be when I grow up!"

"What's that, Scottie?" my mom asked, half-asleep.

"I want to be famous!" I replied.

"That's great," my dad quipped. "But what do you want to be famous *for*?"

I replied, "I want to be famous . . . for writing something!"

(This absolutely happened. My parents can vouch for me.)

Looking back, *that* was a defining moment in my life. An empowering belief (e.g., mental agreement) was formed, and I took actions which eventually led me to uncover the insights in this book. Without this unique and powerful belief in myself and my life's mission, there's *zero* chance I would've had the persistent curiosity to not only acquire these insights, but also to spend the past four years writing this book.

Becoming famous, of course, is no longer my overarching goal. I do, however, burn to see these truths spread far and wide—globally, even—to help change the lives of as many women (and men) as possible, and to assist in the removal of decades and even centuries-old misconceptions regarding a presently out of control gender stereotyping. At this point, I've done everything in my power to bring this about. The path this book is destined to travel from here on out is largely out of my hands, and in the palm of yours.

Online Book Reviews

If you received a *ton* of value from this book, and you'd like to help me advance these life-altering insights, I would greatly appreciate your support in the form of a bold and authentic book review on Amazon.com

Note: If you *do* decide to leave an online review, it would be extremely helpful if you *didn't* use the labels "alpha woman" and "beta man" in your review, or write a summary post, so you don't spoil the surprise for other women. This way they can go through a similar strategic revelation process like you went through and benefit accordingly.

I would also appreciate you helping me spread the word about this book by recommending it to your girlfriends (and possibly some guy friends), posting about it on social media, sharing a video testimonial online, and so on. Together, we can start a grassroots movement that will empower millions of women (and men) to *co-create* their own love stories for everyone's mutual benefit.

Thank you in advance, and best wishes in life and love.

—Scott

A Message for Men

"Help me… help you. Help me, help you."

—JERRY, *JERRY MAGUIRE*

If you would like women to date *you* according to this *New Dating Playbook*, there are many things you can do to help make that happen. You can mention this book on your online dating profile, or bring it up as a fun conversation starter! Post links to this book on social media and all over the Internet. Write a respectful online review. Create a viral video book sharing challenge—whatever it takes to spread these insights as broadly as possible. Collectively, I truly believe we can inspire millions of dynamic women (and men) to make dating great again in a relatively short amount of time.

And remember, as of now, this can be your *New Dating Playbook*, too. So, take the applicable tips and strategies that resonated with you the most, and use them to win the heart, mind, body, and soul of a badass woman who's equally committed to fighting for yours.

A Message for Entrepreneurs, Innovators, World Changers…

"If you want to go fast, go alone.
If you want to go far, go together."

—AFRICAN PROVERB

If you, too, have a passion for changing lives regarding dating and relationships (or marriage), or personal development, and you'd like to discuss ways we could work together—speaking engagements, TV/Podcast appearances, private retreats, perhaps a partnership—please reach out to me.

My extreme "female brain" is *full* of ideas for additional books, products, and services (for women and men) in this category, and beyond. I would love to overcome the limitations of operating solo and utilize my skills as a key member of a winning team. That way we could each focus on our areas of expertise and go further, faster—together.

Lastly, as previously mentioned, I truly believe the collective value of the insights in this book far surpasses the realm of dating and relationships alone. So, if you are an activist, educator, health professional, influencer, or philanthropist—for example—and you'd like to collaborate with me in order to advance these concepts, it would be my honor to work with you.

Website: ScottMcDougal.com

Acknowledgements

To my badass alpha woman editor, Alice Sullivan, thank you for helping me turn my latest manuscript into this book. Without your extremely or mostly "male brain," and your empowered female point of view, as you know, this book would've been much less palatable to my female audience. I couldn't be more pleased and prouder of the work you've done. You were incredible to work with, and I highly recommend your writing and editing services to both women and men.

To my first alpha female editor, Jyssica Schwartz, who initially helped me reorganize my thoughts and concepts, and also helped me translate them from "beta man" language into "alpha woman-friendly" prose, thank you again for your loving patience, insights, and dedication.

Luisa Zhou, you helped me, too. Thank you.

To my alpha female book cover and internal layout designer, Melinda Martin, thank you for helping me create a classy and sexy look and feel in an effort to appeal to as many women as possible, and for working tirelessly to help me present this complex material in a visually beautiful way.

To all the alpha women I've had the privilege of dating, or being in a serious relationship with, thank you for sharing your heart and your life with me. I cherish the good times, and I'm even appreciative for the painful lessons I learned, too. Many of the insights in this book would not have been possible without you.

To my Secret Angel, you lifted me up when I was down, and saved this book by generously supporting my efforts to finish it and publish it. I am forever grateful to you for believing in me and this project, and for your rare love and kindness. Thank you!

To my amazing parents, thank you for loving me unconditionally, for believing in me, and for supporting my dreams and goals no matter how "out there" they might have seemed at times. Also, thank you for raising me to be a Southern gentleman; for teaching me to love and respect others; for reading and helping me edit this book countless times; and for being my best friends.

To all my friends and family who've supported me in innumerable ways, thank you.

To all my doubters, naysayers, critics, frenemies, and haters, you essentially encouraged me to dig deeper and fight harder. Thank you, too!

And to you, dear reader, thank you for purchasing a copy of this book, and for reading and fully considering the concepts within it. I do not know exactly what impact it will have on your love life and overall relationships, but I hope and pray it has given you some measure of clarity, confidence, and power to make your dreams come true. Even if only a few sections or concepts of this book fully resonated with you, great change is heading your way.

The future of dating and relationships is in your hands, Alpha Woman, so lead us well!

About the Author

"Here's to the crazy ones. The misfits. The rebels. The troublemakers. The round pegs in the square holes. The ones who see things differently. They're not fond of rules. And they have no respect for the status quo. You can quote them, disagree with them, glorify or vilify them. About the only thing you can't do is ignore them. Because they change things. They push the human race forward. And while some may see them as the crazy ones, we see genius. Because the people who are crazy enough to think they can change the world, are the ones who do."

—ROB SILTANEN (OFTEN *BELIEVED* TO BE BY STEVE JOBS)

Scott McDougal is a thought leader and changemaker regarding gender psychology in dating and relationships (and marriage), and beyond. His mission is to empower millions of women (and men) to attract, meet, and keep the love of their life. A lifelong dreamer, doer, and strategically creative problem solver, McDougal is also committed to spreading his insights worldwide to help solve applicable interpersonal, business, educational, and societal challenges, as well as to further our current understanding of human history. He believes we each have unique callings and purposes in life, and that we owe it to ourselves and to the world to trust our instincts, push through any fears and insecurities, and make our ambitious dreams come true. With Truth and Love as guiding principles, there's nothing we can't accomplish when we work *together*.

McDougal graduated from Texas Christian University with a Bachelor of Science in Strategic Communication, and from Miami Ad School at Portfolio Center with a graduate certificate in Advertising Copywriting. He enjoys reading books and watching movies about innovative thinkers and world changers. He has a special affinity for romance films, and people watching and analyzing whether they are alpha-dominant, balanced, or beta-dominant (a TV show in which the audience tries to guess which participant is which type would be novel and illuminating). Spare time is spent writing, coaching and consulting, public speaking, playing sports, and walking on the beach.

He also would love to see a series of romance movies made in which women with predominantly "male brains" and men with predominantly "female brains" interact according to this *New Dating Playbook*. It's beyond time for a new wave of romantic love stories!

REFERENCES

Introduction: Truth, Lies, and Love

1 Carman, Judith. 2016. "Singing Our History, Part III: World War II to the Present." Journal of Singing 73 (1): 13.

2 Rosa Parks, Wikipedia, https://en.wikipedia.org/wiki/Rosa_Parks (accessed June 03, 2019).

3 Frantz Fannon, Richard Philcox (translator), *Black Skin, White Masks* (Grove Press; Revised edition (September 10, 2008), https://www.goodreads.com/author/show/37728.

Chapter 1: The Power of Beliefs on Dating

4 Richard Bandler and Garner Thomson, *The Secrets of Being Happy* (The Technology of Health, Hope and Harmony). Copyright, 2011 by Richard Bandler and Garner Thomson, Chapter 5 (p. 109-128).

5 Adam Grant, *Originals: How Non-Conformists Move the World*, Penguin Books, 2016, p. 6.

Chapter 2: The Tale of Two Energies

6 "The Law of Vibration, One Mind One Energy," https://www.one-mind-one-energy.com/Law-of-vibration.html (accessed June 02, 2019).

Chapter 3: The Universal Laws of Attraction

7 "Law of Attraction: The Science of Attracting More of What . . . ," https://www.goodreads.com/book/show/53535.Law_of_Attraction (accessed June 02, 2019).

8 David Deida, *The Way of the Superior Man (A Spiritual Guide to Mastering the Challenges of Women, Work, and Sexual Desires)* (Sounds True, Inc., 1997 and 2004), p. 82.

9 According to Losier, the Law of Attraction is "universal energy around you that obeys the science of physics." *Law of Attraction*, p. 14.

10 The City College of New York, CUNY, Chem 103, Chapter 5.pdf - 5 Thermochemistry 1 5.1 Energy and Energy, https://www.coursehero.com/ file/38849964/Chapter-5pdf/ (accessed June 02, 2019).

11 The Law of Vibration—One Mind One Energy, https://www.one-mind-one-energy.com/Law-of-vibration.html (accessed June 02, 2019).

12 Sonya Rhodes, PhD, with Susan Schneider, *The Alpha Woman Meets Her Match, How Today's Strong Women Can Find Love and Happiness Without Settling* (William Morrow, an imprint of Harper Collins Publishers), p. 7-8.

13 Thomas Umstattd, "The 4000 Year History of Courtship—From Bride Prices to Bundling Beds," May 27, 2015, https://www.thomasumstattd.com/2015/05/ history-of-courtship/.

Chapter 4: Understanding Your Differences

14 John Gray, Ph.D., *Men Are from Mars, Women Are from Venus (The Classic Guide to Understanding the Opposite Sex)* (Quill, a division of Harper Collins, Copyright 1992 by J.G. Productions, Inc), p. 9.

15 Ibid., p. 11.

16 Louann Brizendine, M.D., *The Female Brain*, 2006, p. 4.

17 Including Mark Gungor, Tony Robbins, Dr. John Gray, and others.

18 The quiz is unfortunately no longer available for free but could once be found at https://www.bbc.co.uk/science/humanbody/sex/add_user.shtml.

19 Amber N.V. Ruigrok, et. al., "A Meta-analysis of Sex Differences in Human Brain Structure," *Neuroscience & Biobehavioral Reviews*, Volume 39, February 2014, p. 34-50, https://www.sciencedirect.com/science/article/pii/ S0149763413003011.

20 Christia Spears Brown, PhD, "Everything You Believe Is Wrong: There Is No Such Thing as a Male or Female Brain," 7/24/17, https://www.fastcompany.com/40441920/ everything-you-believe-is-wrong-there-is-no-such-thing-as-a-male-or-female-brain.

21 https://ourworldindata.org/why-do-women-live-longer-than-men

22 U.S. and World Population Clock, United States Census Bureau, https://www. census.gov/popclock/.

23 Dr. Louann Brizendine, *The Male Brain*, p. 53.

24 Dr. Robert A. Glover, *No More Mr. Nice Guy: A Proven Plan for Getting What You Want in Love, Sex, and Life*, Page ix, Copyright 2000, 2003 by Robert Glover, Running Press (Philadelphia, London).

25 Dr. Louann Brizendine, *The Female Brain*, (Harmony; Reprint edition (August 7, 2007), p. 14.

26 Ibid., p. 45.

27 "The Profit: Standard Burger Showdown," November 30, 2015, https://www.cnbc.com/video/2015/11/30/the-profit-standard-burger-showdown-.html.

28 SixWise.com, "How Much of an Advantage Do Tall Men Have? Are Tall Men Really Better Off?" http://www.sixwise.com/newsletters/05/08/03/how_much_of_an_advantage_do_tall_men_have_are_tall_men_really_better_off.htm.

Chapter 5: Change Your Dating Story and Change Your Love Life

29 "Misogyny," https://www.merriam-webster.com/dictionary/misogyny.

30 "Misandry," https://www.merriam-webster.com/dictionary/misandry.

31 Kendra Cherry, "How Confirmation Bias Works," August 8, 2019, https://www.verywellmind.com/what-is-a-confirmation-bias-2795024.

32 Learn more about Katya Varbanova at https://20knation.com.

33 Dr. Brizendine, *The Female Brain*, p. 9.

34 According to the 2013 Census.

35 The Answer Sheet, "Do College Admissions Officers . . . ," http://voices.washingtonpost.com/answer-sheet/college-admissions/how-m.html (accessed June 03, 2019).

36 Tucker Carlson, "Men Seem to Be Becoming Less Male . . . ," https://www.realclearpolitics.com/video/2018/03/08/tucker_carlson_men_seem_to_be (accessed June 03, 2019).

37 "Women Professors: New Challenges for The Next Generation," http://www.nea.org/assets/img/PubAlmanac/Allen_2010.pdf (accessed June 03, 2019).

38 Tucker Carlson, "Men Seem to Be Becoming Less Male."

39 Ibid.

40 Karin Agness Lips, "Don't Buy into The Gender Pay Gap Myth," Forbes.com, April 12, 2016, https://www.forbes.com/sites/karinagness/2016/04/12/dont-buy-into-the-gender-pay-gap-myth/#144fe3aa2596.

41 Dr. Sonya Rhodes, *The Alpha Woman Meets Her Match* (2014), p. 5.

42 "Girls Lead Boys in Academic Achievement Globally," *ScienceDaily.com*, January 26, 2015, https://www.sciencedaily.com/releases/2015/01/150126125015.htm.

43 Alexis Krivkovich, Kelsey Robinson, Irina Starikova, Rachel Valentino, and Lareina Yee, "Women in the Workplace 2017," McKinsey & Company, October 2017, https://www.mckinsey.com/featured-insights/gender-equality/women-in-the-workplace-2017.

44 Dan Rafael, "Floyd Mayweather's purse at $100M; Conor McGregor's $30M biggest of career," *ESPN.com*, August 25,

2017, "http://www.espn.com/boxing/story/_/id/20461204/
floyd-mayweather-guaranteed-100-million-purse-conor-mcgregor-get-30-million.

45 "Conor McGregor Net Worth," CelebrityNetWorth.com, https://
www.celebritynetworth.com/richest-athletes/mma-net-worth/
conor-mcgregor-net-worth/.

46 Oliver Harvey, "Conor McGregor: 'The Secret' Changed My
Life," NYPost.com, July 26, 2017, https://nypost.com/2017/07/26/
conor-mcgregors-rise-from-failed-plumber-to-shocking-superstar/.

47 "Dee Devlin and Conor McGregor's Relationship Timeline," https://www.
irishmirror.ie/sport/dee-devlin-conor-mcgregors-relationship-1029276 (accessed
June 03, 2019).

48 "Who Is Conor McGregor's Girlfriend? Everything You Need to Know,"
https://www.mirror.co.uk/sport/boxing/who-conor-mcgregors-girlfriend-
everything- (accessed June 03, 2019).

49 Quote most frequently attributed to William Johnsen, https://www.amazon.
com/If-Be-Its-Me-Attitude/dp/0938716433.

Chapter 6: The New Dating Playbook for Badass Women

50 "Circadian Rhythms," National Institute of General Medical Sciences, https://
www.nigms.nih.gov/education/pages/factsheet_circadianrhythms.aspx.

Chapter 8: Exchanging Numbers, First Dates, and Beyond

51 Dr. Brizendine, *The Female Brain*, p. xix.
52 Visit https://www.5lovelanguages.com/quizzes/.

Chapter 10: From Commitment to "He Put a Ring on It!"

53 Rick Hanson, Ph.D. with Richard Mendius, MD, *Buddha's Brain: The Practical
Neuroscience of Happiness, Love & Wisdom* (2009: New Harbinger Publications,
Inc.), p. 109-110.